Meatball Sa
Drive Fast And Talk Back To The Cops

By Ronald Roberts

In loving memory of

Margaret Laughlin Roberts
1942-1978

who lived this with me

Other works by Ronald Roberts

"An Anarchist Lullaby" a novel

Haifisch Publications - Lenexa, Kansas

Chapter 1 "Meatball Sangwich"

I grew up in the fifties in the Northeast part of Kansas City, maybe a couple of miles from the "North End" or "Little Italy". It was a baseball cap, Chevrolet, lower middle class and lower class blue collar neighborhood with sporadic, sparse islands of wealth. It had an abundance of corner "Mom and Pop" shops of every description: grocery stores, drug stores with fountains where you could order custom cokes like chocolate or cherry-vanilla, shoe repair shops, clothes stores, anything you could want without a chain store in sight. And most of them were within easy walking distance.

There was a little street off St. John Avenue, the "main drag", called Sunset Drive, where it was rumored that organized crime figures lived. Later, Kansas City Star articles, movies and convictions confirmed this. It was a diverse neighborhood with everything from Italian hucksters, with heavy accents, selling fresh fruit and vegetables out of a pick-up bed, to Sheffield Steel workers, to slick mafia dons in always clean Cadillacs. There were so many Italians in the area, I was thirteen before I realized I wasn't in a minority group. (I'm mostly German with some Cherokee.) Frequently, classmates with Anglo sounding names like Kean, Shores and Wisdom, were half Italian and half Irish. They were all Catholics and if you had to marry outside your race, you should at least marry another Catholic.

No Italian I knew ever said the word sandwich. It was always sangwich with a g. This was driven home repeatedly one summer when, as a college student strapped for a job, I became the ice cream man. My biggest seller was the ice cream sandwich, but no Italian ever asked for anything but an ice cream sangwich. On Morell street, a hefty, swarthy man everyone called Pauly, with a dubious reputation frequently came out and, seeing a group of hungry kids around my truck, would pull out a money clip bulging with a wad of cash, hand me a five and say, "Give 'em whatever they want". I always made sure he got his five dollars worth.

A lunch time staple in the area was delicious meatball sangwiches, and no one, anywhere, ever made one better than Ross DiMaggio at his drive-in "Dairy Way" at Jackson Street and Independence Avenue. Ross was a titan of a man as I recall, 6' 3", at least and probably 275 pounds. His meatball wasn't one of those wussy inch and a half numbers; it was a monster, three and a half to four inches in width, served on a sesame seed bun with the center scooped out to accommodate the behemoth, and slathered with a wonderful spicy red marinara sauce, the recipe for which went back to Sicily. It was a sandwich befitting a man of Ross' dimensions and it was only 35 cents.

The best and biggest sandwich in the universe and it was only 35 cents! Ross built it and they came. Dairy Way started out as a Diary Queen clone, serving soft-serve ice cream in the days before air conditioned homes, when people would line up for a half block on a hot summer night, to cool off with the delightful treat. At first it had an outdoors walk up window where you placed your order. Ross introduced sangwiches and success ensued. Ross built on a vestibule to protect customers from the ever changing Kansas City weather. The gravel parking lot was always full. No date or game was complete without a trip to Dairy Way and a meatball sangwich.

A braggart of a 250 pound Northeast High football player was reputed, on a bet, to have eaten seven. The bet was ten, but he never came close. He lived, but for several hours, he wished he hadn't.

One balmy summer night, two jackasses got into a fight just outside the vestibule. Ross, so furious that he was red in the face, tore off his marinara stained apron and came storming out. He was surprisingly nimble for a man of his size. He grabbed one combatant by the collar and threw him in a northerly direction. He then lifted the other guy by his belt and hurled him south toward Independence Avenue. He then yelled, "Look, you god damned peckerwoods, you're not going to get me shut down. I don't ever want to see either one of you guys here again."

In Ross' world there were only two kinds of people, Italians and peckerwoods.

Being banned from Dairy Way was a dire fate. It not only had the best and cheapest food, it was the center of much of our social life. The huge lot was always full on Fridays and Saturdays with youths milling around talking about the game or comparing new carburetors, recently repaired and primered fenders, or new roll and tuck upholstery. It was where you went to premier your new spinner hub caps or Lake's Pipes. A young man's car, in those days, was a work in progress, a personal statement and the Dairy Way was where you went to flaunt the latest improvements. People came there who never ordered any food. It was the place to be. When one was fortunate, some comely teenager in a pleated skirt, sweater and saddle oxfords, would let you buy her a meatball sangwich and then sit in your car with you while she ate it. If you were really lucky, you got her phone number and a date next week-end, which included, of course, a trip to the Dairy Way and another meatball sangwich.

I was there so often, Ross knew me by name. As I would stroll up to the counter, Ross would yell, "One meatball sangwich" to the cook.

I had this great friend in those days, E. Floyd Connerley Jr. He was every underclassman's ideal big brother, always there for a ride to the game or just to get a sandwich, which was pretty much what we lived on. He knew a bunch or cute girls and could always round you up a date for an event. He was a ruddy faced 200 pound hunk of Irishman with curly black hair combed straight back, dancing blue eyes and a perpetual huge smile. He even had E. Floyd emblazoned on his blue and gold Benton Literary Society jacket which he wore everywhere. The literary societies were a front for high school fraternities and sororities which had been banned by the Board of Education. Our primary activity was concocting pranks and practical jokes to perpetrate on the other literary societies. Most of our members didn't know Ernest Hemingway from J. D. Salinger. Floyd had a pale metallic green James Dean '49 Mercury, like in "Rebel Without a Cause" - well, maybe not quite like James Dean. Floyd's was the four door model and had rusted out rocker panels. E. Floyd was the only man on earth who liked meatball sangwiches more than I did.

We were all fond of the dirt track jalopy races every Saturday night at the old Riverside Stadium, which was just off the Missouri river in a town called Riverside, adjacent to Kansas City in Northwesterly direction. Riverside was famous for three things - floods, a cut rate liquor store called the Red X and the stadium. We were lucky that summer, there was no flood. Every time it rained really hard Riverside had high water and the stadium was closed till the high water subsided. Floyd would call and round up a car full of guys who wanted to see the races every Saturday night. I was always ready as was my younger brother, Terry. We'd pile in Floyd's Merc, usually six of us, three in the front and three in the back. (The only cars with bucket seats back then were the English two seaters which no one in my world could afford. Cars were utilitarian, for getting you to work and transporting your family and not for "sports".) We'd make the drive over to Riverside, find a place to park, usually about six blocks away, and trek in. The next order of business was a hot dog and a coke to tide us always hungry teenagers over till we could hit the Dairy Way. There were two dominant drivers in those days, Junior Hower, who could tune a flathead Ford better than anyone on the planet (He regularly beat Corvette powered Super Modifieds with this obsolete engine) and Bud Hunacutt. E. Floyd loved Bud Hunacutt. E. Floyd also liked to gamble just a bit and he would bet the entire carload a meatball sangwich on Bud Hunacutt. We got all the other drivers, he got Bud Hunacutt! This was the summer of Junior Hower's amazing winning streak. Each week was like a re-run with Junior's red and white number 24 roaring across the finish line, taking the checkered flag, headers spewing fire, while narrowly nipping the always game Bud Hunacutt at the finish line. This happened ten

weeks in a row, and being a man of his word, E. Floyd not only supplied the transportation, but he also ponied up for five or six meatball sangwiches. The eleventh race started just like all the others with Junior winning his heat race and the trophy dash, which meant he had to start the feature at the back of the pack. They had an inverted starting order with the slowest starting first and the fastest starting last. This never slowed him down. Junior drove with a fury, moving up rapidly. Usually, by the fifth lap, he had passed everyone and was in first. That night he was right on schedule, passing one car in the first turn and another on the second, his massive rear tires spraying tiny pellets of mud onto the protective screen, as he roared past, blue flames flashing from his exhaust. By the second lap he was drafting, right on Hunacutt's back bumper. It took him two laps, but Junior got high on turn three and cut Bud off, thundering down the straight, a red and white missile. Win number eleven appeared certain as Junior streaked by the grandstand. The fans were standing and yelling at peak volume in unanimous tribute when disaster struck. Junior's red and white #24 slowed unexplainably, sputtered, and coasted into the pits. His perfect flathead had let him down. Junior climbed out through the window, took off his helmet and we knew it was over. All great winning streaks end at some point, but the summer of 1959, Junior Hower was the man every teenage boy wanted to be.

I thought E. Floyd would throw a valve! He leaped into the air, getting hang time Michael Jordan would have been proud of, and cheered boisterously as our hearts sunk. Bud Hunacutt's Blue jalopy roared across the finish line, breaking Junior's streak. Bud jumped out of his car, and threw his fist in the air. At last he had defeated his nemesis. Bud got his trophy and put a serious lip lock on the shapely model that had presented it, something Junior wouldn't do. He never kissed the models. It was assumed that Mrs. Hower wouldn't have approved. The crowd usually booed junior for this act of fidelity, but never me. I respected it. E. Floyd was all smiles as we glumly walked to the lot. "What did you guys think of that" he chided? My brother
Terry, who always hated to lose at anything, pointed out that Hunacutt was, yet again, behind when Junior's engine had blown. We all got in his Merc and E. Floyd cranked his radio up to ear bleed as Chuck Berry wailed "Maybalene, why can't you be true?" We cruised across the ASB bridge, turned left at Admiral and headed for the Dairy Way. The lot was so full we could hardly find a place to park. Everyone was gathered around John Glorioso's candy pearl white '40 Chevy hot rod with the

gorgeous maroon pin stripping job and the full chrome Corvette engine with two four barrels. John's family was one of the sporadic, sparse islands of wealth. We made our way to the long line and waited patiently for the inevitable - having to buy E. Floyd five meatball sangwiches. One at a time, we completed our task and E. Floyd had five. He foolishly, but courageously, declared his intention to eat all of them! We, in unison, shook our heads in disbelief at this folly. He powered through the first one rapidly with a belch that rattled the glass in the vestibule, then attacked the second, which presented no apparent problem. Half- way through the third, he realized the ridiculousness of his *braggadocio*. He had hit the wall! He started looking really queasy as he struggled through meatball number three. He then, with an embarrassed grin, wrapped them in a paper napkin, and realizing he had been just a bit hasty, stated he would save them for later. We all went by John's '40 Chevy to pay tribute, congratulating him on his two touchdown game as wing back for our Northeast Vikings, and went home.

Scroll forward five years and I have become a college dropout for the first time. (There would be a third and final time.) I was coming in off the road after a brief tour, playing upright bass with a moderately successful folk singer named Bill Brown. The Beatles had recently been on the Ed Sullivan Show and rocked the world. The demise of the folk fad was at hand. My family had moved to the extreme south part of Kansas City, but my fiancé, Margaret, was still a Northeast girl. The first thing I did, on my return, was drive my metallic blue '54 Ford over to her house, pick her up and cruise on down to the Dairy Way. When we got there, my heart was broken. The Dairy Way was boarded up with a closed sign nailed to the entrance. How could this be? What were Ross and his family going to do? I looked around and saw a McDonald's in one direction and a Smack's (A short lived local McDonald's clone) in the other. Tasteless, plastic, corporate food had reared its ugly head, replacing the little mom and pop shops. Instead of families making a living with unique food, often indigenous to their ethnic background, you had rich guys buying multiple franchises!

Fast forward thirty more years, and I'm a college dropout for good, walking down the main street of Amsterdam. A sculptor friend had obtained a grant and I was the electronic music composer part of a three artist European tour. We were looking for a good place to have a quaint Dutch lunch and, seeking less expensive fare, we abandoned the thoroughfare that was full of tourist traps. We turned down a little side street, and there, to our amazement, all in a row, were a McDonald's, a Pizza Hut and a Burger King! Sometimes progress really stinks! I am seldom sympathetic with anything French, but perhaps they have the right idea in legislating against these cultural beachheads.

If I had a time machine, I would set it for 1959, head for Northeast Kansas City, drive to the Dairy Way, say hello to Ross, and order myself a meatball sangwich.

Epilogue

In the midst of an early evening nap, I was awakened by the telephone. I didn't get up in time to catch the call, but there, on my answering machine, was E. Floyd Connerley Jr! I hadn't seen him in 37years! We arranged a reunion with E. Floyd and the Roberts brothers. Floyd no

longer drives a Mercury, but Terry does, a 2002 loaded silver Grand Marquis that is his pride and joy. And that's what we rode in as we drove over to the Marco Polo, a little Italian *trottoria* that is the closest thing I could think of to the Dairy Way. As we pulled into the lot, there, standing in front of the place was E. Floyd Connerley Jr., His curly hair now gray, and he was a little heavier, but his blue Irish eyes still danced. Terry yelled, "Come on, Junior Hower" as we drove by and found a parking place.

It was meatball sangwiches all around, and the Marco Polo has a great one called the "Gondola". Thomas Wolfe said, "You Can't Go Home Again", but that day we came close!

Chapter 2 “My Big Pro Debut”

My grandfather, Charlie Slankard, (his name was Charlie not Charles, and he had no middle name) was the quintessential “good time Charlie”. Wherever there was country music, booze and people to party with, he was there also! Calling him the life of the party would have been a gross understatement. He was the party - born to celebrate! Charlie was a German/American “Okie” farmer who had it rough, like nearly everyone in Oklahoma, during the great depression. A massive drought made farming an impossible proposition. I well remember my angel of a mother, Fern Marie Slankard Roberts, telling me how, at one point, the family had nothing to eat but potatoes for nearly a year, and how she put cardboard in her shoes to cover the holes so she could walk to school. Many of my family, Slankards and Zerbes, were Steinbeck “Grapes of Wrath” people who put everything they owned on the back of a flatbed truck and drove through the Arizona desert to California, to Fresno and Salinas to pick grapes. Always the iconoclast, Charlie went against the grain and hung on till 1936. He survived by driving a produce truck for his successful older brother, Owen (pronounced Own), who lived in San Antonio (pronounced San Antone), and had a little side business, bootlegging hooch. Oklahoma was a curiosity where alcohol was concerned. With a population dominated by fundamentalist Baptists, some counties were dry, the sale of liquor was prohibited, and some were wet. There, you could get hammered at will. The greater Tulsa area was dry, so Charlie, always the clever opportunist, quickly figured out he could buy booze in Kansas City at the turn around point on his route, hide it in the truck's undercarriage in case he got pulled over and inspected by the law, and double his money back in Tulsa selling it to tipplers, provided he could keep from drinking up the profits. Grandpa was a Baptist on Sundays and a hedonist on the other six days.

In 1936, against all odds, Charlie got a job working for the railroad and moved his family to Kansas City. In 1944, my Dad joined the Army as World War II was beginning to wind down. There was no longer any doubt about the result, in Europe or in the Pacific. We lived in a second floor walk-up over a tavern at 17th and Summit, an area referred to as the "West Side". It was a three generation arrangement. There were seven of us in the four room apartment; Grandpa, Grandma, Uncles Wesley and Clarence, Mom, my brother Terry and me. I recall the dark wood floors I used to play on with my favorite toy, an olive drab wooden model Jeep that my Dad had sent me. It seemed large at the time, but I was only three. I also remember the old toilet with the water tank high up on the wall with a chain you pulled to flush it. I loved going for walks with my Mom, especially when the air was filled with four engine bombers, a frequent occurrence. There were so many and it was so loud you could feel the vibrations. Boeing Aircraft, manufacturer of the venerable B-17 Flying Fortress, was located in Wichita, and Kansas City must have been right on the way to their delivery point.

The downside of our apartment was that it was right above Grandpa's favorite "beer joint" as Grandma would say. It made it far too easy for Charlie to blow his paycheck letting the good times roll!

The West Side was a poor neighborhood populated predominately by Mexicans. I loved hearing the lively polkas waft from the radios in the neighboring houses, the brightly colored clothing they wore and the wonderful tamales my Uncle Clarence would bring home. We had a big console radio and on Saturdays we would all gather around and listen to "The Grand Old Opry", from Nashville, Tennessee. In the top compartment of the big radio was a record player that played big thick, hard wax 78 rpm discs that broke easily. In retrospect, I was obviously born to the music. I spent my days listening to Gene Autry singing "Back In the Saddle Again", Ernest Tubbs' "Walkin' the Floor Over You", Eddie Arnold's "If I Had a Nickel" and "Little Jimmy" Dickens wailing "Take An Old Cold Tater and Wait" on scratchy, noisy purple labeled "Okeh" records. Country was the only music I had access to. Grandpa played the fiddle and I loved it, especially when he'd set me on his lap, put my hand on the bow, and let me think I was playing. I already knew, full well, that music was to be my destiny. He would teach me the words to his favorite tunes and have me and my brother sing along, (a liability in that Terry never had any singing talent and just muttered along in a monotone). I was blessed with an unusually good memory and by the age of 4, I already had a respectable repertoire.

When I was not listening to music, and loving art, I would try to draw musical instruments and cowboy singers with my crayons. It was quite futile. Terry got the art talent and I got the music.

My Mom worked at Eisen's Dry Goods store in the north end by the city market because it was close enough to walk and we couldn't afford the daily bus fare. Grandpa had lucked into a job at the Santa Fe Railroad by virtue of the fact that every able bodied man of draft age was in the army. Wes was in high school, Clarence in grade school, and Grandma, Clara Freda Zerbe Slankard, a treasure in every sense of the word, took care of Terry and me, cooked and did the domestic chores. I really enjoyed her singing as she ironed - "Way down yonder in the Indian nation, just about a mile from the reservation, in the Oklahoma hills where I was born" (An old Woody Guthrie tune). Mom didn't make much at Eisen's, but we did get a small allotment from Dad. Grandma had to be on duty every Friday night to guard the family food supply. She would post herself at the front door of the tavern to intercept Charlie before he got inside, or he would have blown it all, buying drinks for the house! Once he had had a few, he lost all contact with reality and he'd be feeding the juke box, singing and dancing like a whirling dervish, everyone's long lost pal. Grandpa was, at heart, a musician, but he never got the chance to pursue it as a profession. Professional musician didn't exist as an occupation in the depression ravaged Oklahoma. He was a part time drunk because he lacked the wherewithal to indulge himself full- time. With Grandpa's coaching, I soon became a fairly proficient little country singer, blending

my voice with his mellow fiddle. One day, as he came home form work, Grandpa had a bright idea. He picked me up and without telling anyone, took me down to the tavern and started dropping nickels into the juke box. He set me at the end of the bar and had me singing along at the top volume of my boy soprano voice capability, "If I had a nickel, I know what I would do, spend it all for candy, and give it all to you, that's how much I love you, baby." (I still remember the lyrics he taught me over sixty years later.) I was a big hit with the resident drunks and they started giving me change. Grandpa went and got a beer mug for me to keep my earnings in. Quite the little ham, I was having a great time being the center of attention and getting my first taste of a live audience. After a while, Mom came home from work and not finding me, was terrified and started screaming "Where's Ronnie?" Grandma told her I was with Charlie. Now after years of seeing first hand, the havoc that alcoholism can wreak on a poor family, Mom, never at any point in her life had any tolerance for drinking. I have read this is a frequent trait in children of alcoholics. Mom had little doubt where Charlie was and headed straight for the beer joint! She saw me sitting on the bar and was furious. After all, I was seriously under age! She stormed across the dance floor, screaming at her father, grabbed me and started stomping out. Grandpa handed her the mug and said, "Here, take the kid's money. He earned it." Mom was always slow to anger, but when she finally got there, it would register on a seismograph. She hurled the beer mug straight at Charlie's head, but the glass was high and wide. My take was scattered all over the floor. Mom never had much of a pitching arm. (Neither did I. It was a family trait.) At four, I already knew that silver could be exchanged for candy and ice cream at the little confectionary on the next corner. Feeling my loss deeply, I began to cry triple *forte*. It was to no avail. Mom had no intention of allowing her little boy to become the world's youngest cabaret singer and that was the end of that! My music career was going to have to wait eleven years till I became the bass fiddle player in "Harold's Krackerjacks", a fifties rock'n roll band in

Raytown, Missouri. For all his shortcomings, I really loved Grandpa. What I saw was a man who had an extraordinary ability to enjoy himself and I did not see his failure to ever be serious about anything as a fault. Time has taught me that serious is often not what its cracked up to be. My friend of over fifty years, the great multi-instrumentalist, Mike

Perryman, once told me that I could enjoy myself better than anyone he knew. That was a gift from Charlie to me. (Fortunately, I always had mom's attitude toward alcohol.) I was not to have Charlie much longer. He was never happy in Kansas City. He was an Okie and needed the red dirt of home.

Missing his brother, one day on a whim, he decided to hitchhike to Tulsa. His life ended in 1946 on Highway 71 where he was found by the side of the road, having been struck and killed by a hit-and-run driver. Dad was out of the army by then and I recall all of us all piling into the 1946 maroon Ford four door sedan he had rented for the trip to Tulsa, and motoring out Highway 71, through Grandview, over the two lane blacktop, on to Tulsa. Grandpa was back in Oklahoma where he belonged.

Twenty four years later, I had followed my calling and was a reasonably successful jazz bassist and composer with my own concert ensemble. In tribute to my first musical influence, I had penned a piece called "Oklahoma Blues For Old Charlie". It would become a concert ensemble staple, performed at every concert for over thirty years and part of my first album.

In 1997, fifty-one years after Grandpa's fatal accident, Mom, now in her seventies, was going to fly down to Tulsa to visit relatives. I hadn't been down there in many years, and wanting to see my cousin Geraldine, who was the same age as my Mom, I decided to drive Mom down there while there was still some of my family alive to see. Mom, Gerry and I went out to the old Broken Arrow Cemetery where Charlie was buried. Mom said she remembered Charlie was on the last row, but I pointed out how long ago that had been, and the little village of Broken Arrow had become a thriving suburb of Tulsa. The three of us split up to cover more ground and searched for Charlie's grave. As if "Old Charlie" were calling out to me through time, there in front of me was a shiny brass grave marker reading "Charlie Slankard 1893 -1946." The memories came back like a tidal wave as I remembered our all too brief time together. Tears flowed as I thought about how I had followed in his footsteps and had become the musician he had wanted so much to be. I felt he would have been very proud of me. If only he could have tapped his foot, counted off Roy Acuff's "Wabash Cannonball", his favorite, and we could have played together!

They say that time heals all wounds, but I don't think so. We just learn to live with our losses. We realize that it hurts too much to continue to live back there, there is nothing we can do, and just move on. But the feeling of loss never goes away.

Mom and me 1944

Chapter 3 "Our First House"

Dad's getting out of the Army had a real effect on our life style. As a former soldier, he had the "G. I bill of rights". President Roosevelt's programs had made for profound changes in the lives of poor people, and we were, most definitely, charter members of that club. The G. I. Bill afforded returning veterans a chance to own their own homes by guaranteeing small interest loans. My Dad got one and it was goodbye 17th & Summit and hello 2501 Bellefontaine. Dad had also found employment as a bus driver for Kansas City Public Service.

We moved into the 19th century wood frame house with windows that were trimmed in leaded stained glass, with a big yard and steep back stairway. The beefy, hairy ice man in a sleeveless undershirt which today is called a "wife beater", would grab the big blocks of ice with his tongs, sweating, as he lugged them up those stairs. Though refrigerators had been around since the thirties, they were well beyond our means. We had an oak ice box. We were just happy to have our own house. It was a big step. We were no longer lower class, we were lower middle class.

I was ebullient at having an actual yard and we had so much more space. It was the same deal, Grandpa, Grandma, Wes and Clarence were still with us, but Wes was not there for long. He had graduated, not a frequent occurrence in our family at that time, and it wouldn't be too long before he got married and moved to an apartment of his own. My Dad also bought a used '41 Ford woody wagon! We had a house and a car! Would the avalanche of good fortune ever stop? Terry and I were in heaven.

Our happy home was short-lived. Grandpa was killed in the accident and shortly after that, we began to hear concern about the fact that an African/American family had moved in up the street. The races were totally separated in those days, with black people having their own city within a city. There was a hyphenated name for it which decorum and social conscience preclude me from using. They patronized their own restaurants, theaters, grocery stores, and drug stores because they were refused service in ours. Mom and Dad were neither well educated nor sophisticated. They had both dropped out of high school in their freshman year. They simply needed to work if they were going to eat. Not only was every cent they had invested in that house, they also had a substantial mortgage. A ruthless real estate agent started scaring the hell out of the residents, telling them that the neighborhood was turning and their property would be worthless. This deplorable tactic was called "block busting". The real estate companies would buy up properties on the cheap and sell them at inflated prices to African/Americans who were simply trying to better their lives. My folks were terrified. My Dad always had a good sense of survival and he cleverly negotiated a deal which got us out of that house and into 211 South Monroe, out Northeast as they used to say. A real estate agent had assured them that there would be no blacks in that area because the mafia would never permit it. (This was true during the 13 years I lived there. The rumor was that the mafia had decreed that there would be no blacks north of Independence Avenue nor east of The Paseo. They not only were willing to enforce this edict, they knew how! In my Northeast High School graduating class of 1960, there were 389 of us, none of them black.)

Our new old house was a forty year improvement over its predecessor. My Dad had also ditched the Ford and bought a spiffy black 1947 Chevrolet Fleetline. We were moving up in the world. He never in his life hesitated the slightest in maxing out his credit. And Mom got her first refrigerator, a General Electric. We made home brew popsicles in the summer with Cool Aid and frozen vegetables were so much better than canned. It had a perfect record for over forty years, never having to be repaired even once. Mom loved it so much she couldn't give it up. When we moved to better digs and got a new and improved model, it went with us. The old G. E. just moved into the garage where it cooled soda pop and beer. It was still working when Mom and Dad, wanting a simpler life because of advancing age, gave up their house for an apartment and sold it at a garage sale in 1992.

Our house was a two bedroom, two story, white stucco covered unit with an L shaped wrap around porch that was great on rainy days. Mom and Dad got one bedroom, Grandma, Terry and I shared the other and Clarence slept on an army cot in the hall between the two. Wes had joined the Navy. The house was between Independence Avenue and St. John. Terry and I delighted in our new world. We had a big back yard with cherry trees and there were many children of our age in the area. We also were just a few feet from an alley which was a wondrous adventure, ripe with potential.

Dad's tenure as a bus driver was short. He had a background in boxing and a hair-trigger temper, not a good combination. A drunk had gotten on the bus and not paid. My Dad grabbed him and told him to either drop a coin in the slot or get off. According to my Dad, the drunk called him a son-of-a-bitch, something Dad would never tolerate, and then took an ill advised swing at him. Dad threw the right hand that had knocked several Golden Gloves opponents out. He chalked up another K.O., then, picked the drunk up and threw him off the bus. The drunk took umbrage at this and hired a sleazy lawyer who sued the bus company. Then Dad got fired. This was a blessing in disguise in that Dad began his career as a salesman, something he enjoyed and excelled at. He became a road man for "The Book of Knowledge" selling encyclopedias in small towns.

In 1948, I began my education at the Scarrit Elementary school and settled in for 13 years of life as a Northeast resident.

Dad Mom Terry and Me 1945

Chapter 4 "Hopalong"

My family got their first television in the spring of 1950. My Dad had an intense dedication to boxing all of his life. He hadn't gotten very far in the sport and had left it behind like a worn out suitcase before I was born. There was nothing he could do about his short arms which are a curse for a fighter and a Roberts' family trait. But the pugilism fire in him never went out. When he discovered that there was a "Gillette Cavalcade of Sports" boxing program on television, all semblance of reason was quickly jettisoned. In spite of being in debt up to his eyebrows with the house and the '47 Chevy, he spent all day Saturday on the telephone and finally found a department store, Gorman's, on Minnesota Avenue in Kansas City, Kansas, that would give him a revolving charge account and that was it! We immediately adjourned to the black Chevy and crossed the Inter-City Viaduct in short order. We returned with the electronic marvel, a tiny Motorola with a 10" screen. It got a place of honor in the living room against the west wall, crowned by its ungainly antennae called "rabbit ears", and nights with "Amos 'n Andy" and "I love Lucy" began. There was only one channel, WDAF, channel 4, and they didn't even broadcast all day. But Terry and I were so enthralled that we would get up early on Saturday and sit and watch the test pattern till the programs began. A new world of wonders was now at our fingertips - Howdy Doody, Buffalo Bob, Clarabelle the clown who was always squirting people with his seltzer bottle, and a creature that appeared to have been created from the biological spare parts bin, Flubadub. Buffalo Bob and Clarabelle were real people while the others were well designed marionettes. Television was our passport to the past with the Johnny Mack Brown Kit Carson western serials, and a glimpse of the future with Larry "Buster" Crabbe, a former Olympic swimmer portraying both Flash Gordon and Buck Rogers spacemen! We waited impatiently for each Saturday to come when we could see the next episode where Buck or Flash would, once again, manage another miraculous escape from what appeared to be certain death. But to us, the undisputed king of TV was William Boyd as Hopalong Cassidy, with his tall black hat with the Tom Mix crease, black shirt with a bolo tie and twin pearl handled Colt .45's at his side with leather thongs tied around each leg to facilitate lightning fast draws with both hands. He sat, majestically, atop Topper, an immense snow white stallion that was the most beautiful horse I had ever seen. His comedic side kick, the always hungry, California, was played by the heavily mustached Andy Clyde. Young Lucky completed this fearless trio. We were such Cassidy fans that when we got a cocker spaniel puppy, Terry and I wanted to name him Hopalong, but Mom said that wasn't a good name for a dog so we compromised with Lucky. As poor Lucky would soon survive being hit by a dump truck and becoming an amputee (right front), Hopalong would have been an ironic moniker. (The guys we played baseball with dubbed him "Tripod".)

William Boyd was an astute business man. When filming ceased in the forties, the studio didn't see any value to what they considered an obsolete character, but Boyd did. He loved playing Hopalong because he was a man's man and a welcome relief from the effete soap opera roles he had played heretofore, and he saw television looming. He bought out all rights to the Hopalong Cassidy character and also the masters to all 28 films. Then a few years later, TV began its assault on the movie industry and showing old films was considerably less expensive than creating new programming. There was a ready market for Hopalong, cleverly syndicated by Boyd. He made $800,000 off Hoppy movies in 1950 at a time when a really nice new car could be had for $1,500!

From the vantage point of our TV set, it was obvious to us that singing cowboys were for sissies. Any fool knew that there was no time to stop and sing as you branded doggies or chased

down and apprehended evil rustlers. Hopalong was the top dog and the man every boy wanted to be, brave, honest and true. During the week, I would procure the Saturday essentials from Agron's Market at Askew and St. John - a couple of bottles of Nehi strawberry, and a bag of Brach's "Michigan Cherries" candy - then settle in for a perfect winter's day of old western movies on television. We'd wait impatiently for the showing of another 1930's film of Hoppy's adventures. (The first of the 28 films was made in 1934.) It was seventy minutes of heaven! Mom was forbidden to buy any brand of bread but Butternut because they sponsored Hopalong's show. Wonder Bread may have built strong bodies eight ways, but we were confirmed Butternut men. The old movies became so popular that they spawned a new television series and new episodes were filmed. Seemingly, all at once, Hopalong was ubiquitous. The downtown dime stores, Kressge's, T G & Y and Woolworth's were flooded with inexpensive Hoppy paraphernalia - lunch pails, black hats, black shirts, cap pistols, boots, spurs - I still have my Hopalong Cassidy cocoa mug! My oldest friend, my brother-in-law, Jim Sander, said he actually had Hopalong Cassidy wall paper in his bedroom!

Before television, neighborhood movie theaters abounded. There were seven within easy access from our house. Four, the Gladstone, Benton, Vista and one for which the name I can't recall on St.John Avenue, were in easy walking distance. The Belmont and

National were just a short ride on the bus, which was just a dime for kids. They began fighting back against the TV onslaught. Tired of seeing empty houses instead of free spending, hungry kids, the Vista, at Independence Avenue and Prospect, went all in. For a mere ten cents, you could view two full length Hopalong Cassidy full length features, plus 12 great Warner Brothers cartoons! What a bonanza! That was one more movie and 12 cartoons more then you got on TV! Hopalong along with Tweety, Sylvester, Bugs Bunny… we hounded mom till she let us go. Because of a particularly cold winter, we took the Independence Avenue trolley bus. (Mom didn't learn to drive till 1953.) Mom wondered how they could make any money with just a ten cent admission charge. She missed the obvious - grossly overpriced concessions. We got off the bus, bought our tickets, and joined the stampede. Nearly every seat was filled with hungry kids who would be there for over three hours. What better way to spent a cold winter's day? Mom, because of a limited budget and the ridiculously over inflated prices, limited us to one treat and one soft drink apiece. The lights went down, the movie started and the audience was spellbound. We all cheered as Hopalong meted out much needed justice to the bad guys. After the cartoons, we hustled out to the lobby to select our snack, braving the tumult of hungry kids that was lined up nearly out to the entrance. They couldn't pop the popcorn fast enough. The Vista had a coin operated soft drink dispenser that fascinated me. It was worth a dime just to see it work. You inserted your coin and a paper cup came down, then you depressed the button of your preference, then flavored syrup came out in one squirt and carbonated water in another, mixing your drink right before your eyes. I always chose burgundy, which was really just plain grape soda. Then I picked Bon Bons, little chocolate covered ice cream nuggets lined up in a row in the paper box. We got back to our seats just in time. There were more cartoons. Wiley Coyote got crushed, once again, with an anvil from the Acme Anvil Company, Bugs ate all of Elmer Fudd's "cawwots", and Tweety "Tot I saw a puddy tat"! Then there was a surprise. The ticket stubs were numbered and they held a drawing for Hopalong Cassidy merchandise. I carefully watched my stub, but came up craps. I watched other kids getting free hats, spurs, cap pistols, and comic books. However, just when we thought all was lost, Terry's number came up and he won a short sleeve, dark green and white sweater with Hoppy's smiling countenance covering the chest. Terry was always lucky. He was in heaven! Mom, seeing my disappointment, later bought me one like Terry's at Woolworth's. The second feature started and, once again, Hopalong waylaid the bad guys. I thought it was funny that Hoppy shot Robert

Mitchum, who had become a big movie star since these low budget movies had been made, in both of the movies that day.

Hopalong Cassidy was more realistic than the other westerns. He didn't spontaneously burst into song, accompanied by a suddenly appearing out of nowhere ensemble, and he didn't pull off any impossible shots like Roy Rogers shooting the gun out of someone's hand. When someone shot at Hoppy, he did the only sensible thing - took dead aim and canceled the scoundrel's ticket. Early in the series, Hopalong was a vagabond former Federal Marshall, roaming the range with his two sidekicks, looking for a place to settle. In subsequent movies, he found his place and established the Bar-20 cattle ranch. From then on, he was always a working rancher. The plots were always believable, with issues that were likely to confront a working western businessman - rustlers, water rights, land grabs... As a part Cherokee, one of the things I liked about Hopalong movies was that Native Americans were not portrayed as bloodthirsty howling savages. They were depicted as a dignified people with their own culture.

The last time I saw Hoppy was as a 12 year old Boy Scout at the annual American Royal parade. I watched the horses, marching bands and convertible riding celebrities go by as I scarfed my lunch, a couple of Jim's tamales that I had bought from a street vendor's cart. Finally, right in front of me, was Hopalong Cassidy, regal in black and silver, atop noble gleaming white Topper, a fine sight to see! I waved to Hoppy as he rode by and I'll swear, he looked right at me, smiled and waved back. That was my farewell to Hoppy. I was growing up. My new hero was the switch hitting New York Yankee's slugger, Mickey Mantle, whom I had watched play in the American Association league for our Kansas City Blues at Municipal Stadium while he was a young minor leaguer.

Doing research for the piece, I recently watched an old Hopalong movie that I have on a VHS video cassette. I was surprised at how well made it was. A stubble faced Bob Mitchum got plugged, yet again, but this time not by Hoppy, but by an evil land grabbing banker. I also, not too long ago, saw a Turner Classic Movies documentary on William Boyd as Hoppy. Topper was really his horse and lived to be over thirty. Boyd loved the Hoppy character and frequently appeared in parades as Cassidy. His last parade was when Topper went to the big grasslands in the sky. Boyd said he just couldn't continue without him. In his later years, Boyd refused to be photographed because he wanted to be remembered as Hopalong, who was a fine hero for a young lad. Unlike most of today's celebrities, Boyd led a quiet family life, disdaining excess, avarice and bad publicity, and was always mild mannered and kind to animals. Where is Hoplong when we really need him?

Terry and Me in our Hoppy shirts

Chapter 5 "My Dog Lucky"

When I was 6 and my brother 5, after much urging, our parents got us a puppy. My Uncle Clarence had a friend who raised Cocker Spaniels and he talked her into giving us a little black and white fellow who was the runt of the litter. He was a cute little guy with very curly fur and enormous long ears that he often tripped over when he ran. A heated discussion ensued over a proper handle for the pup. Terry and I wanted Hopalong. Mom nixed this. Next we wanted Dagwood. Our next door neighbors, Denver and Virginia Maddox, had a buff colored female cocker named Blondie, so we thought they could be Dagwood and Blondie like the popular comic strip. Again we were overruled. Mom said she had read that dog names should end in ie because that was easy for them to understand, so we finally agreed on Lucky, after Hopalong's sidekick. Terry was very disappointed so Mom suggested that his middle name could be Dagwood. When I was a boy, I had several food quirks, one of which was bread crusts, which I never, under any circumstances, ever ate. The remains of my morning toast became Lucky's favorite food. He went nuts when I threw them to him on the back porch. Our boyhood logic dictated that since Lucky had a middle name, he should have a last name too. We named him after his favorite food. He became Lucky Dagwood Toast.

He had a typical puppy-hood, chewing on shoes, peeing on the floor and ingesting anything he could get into his mouth. He really became our pal. Lucky, Terry and I were the "Three Musketeers". He went everywhere with us except to school. He would wait on the front porch and come scampering up when we came home.

When he was about six months old, we called him and he didn't come, which was highly unusual. He always associated his name with impending food and being perpetually hungry, responded promptly. I went out to look for him and became very distraught when I couldn't find him anywhere. Then I saw a black and white lump lying in the street at the intersection on Monroe and Anderson. Fearing the worst, I ran like a cheetah. Lucky was a bloody unconscious mess. I carried him back up to the house as the tears streamed down my young cheeks. He came to and started whimpering. Mom called Dad who rushed home and took him to the vet. (We only had one car and no other way to get him help.) Terry and I were heartsick. We soon learned that Lucky had sustained serious injuries, a crushed right front leg, a broken jaw and had lost most of his teeth. Dad called and said that the vet had said we should probably put him down. Terry and I cried so hard that he just couldn't do it. The doctor had not taken into account Lucky's great fighting heart! Lucky was in the Northeast Pet Hospital for about a week. When he came home, he had a wire in his jaw that would be there for life, and his paralyzed right front leg was all taped up and dangled uselessly. The vet said we should give it six months. If Lucky was to regain any feeling in it, which sometimes happened, it would transpire within that time. This failing to occur, the leg should be amputated. Six months came and went with no improvement so the surgery was performed. Lucky was very young and adopted to being tripedal very quickly. He would follow us everywhere - up to Kosmiki's Drug Store on St. John to get a vanilla coke and a pack of Topps' baseball cards with five cards and a big pink block of bubblegum for five cents, or to the vacant lot at Morrell and Monroe where we played baseball. It wasn't like today where there is an abundance of parks with baseball fields - we had to improvise. A large elm tree was first base, we implemented a rock for second and a telephone pole was third. We drew home plate in the dirt with a stick. There was a game on most of the time that one could join with the Woody brothers, Jimmy and Jerry, Chuck Tie, Bob and Dominic Messina, Richard Sircco, Pat and Mike McNamara, and Anton "Dutch" Sol-Daniels being the mainstays. I had a McGregor "Ted Kluzewski" model first baseman's mitt and a 'Whitey Lockman" model Louisville Slugger bat that I had gotten for Christmas that year. If there was no game on at the vacant lot, we would adjourn to the Scarritt School playground where there was a different bunch of kids - Tommy Larabee, the Ferhwalt brothers, Larry Burghoff, Johnny Buffa and Melchor Nunez, among others. This was second choice because we much preferred playing on dirt rather than the asphalt of the playground where a wicked groud ball could be a life changing experience. A bad hop could inflict painful damage, like a chipped tooth or a shiner. The worst case happened to Bernie Fehrwalt. It got him right in the testicles and he lay right where he fell, writhing in pain for about ten minutes.

Our best friend was Chuck Tye, and wanting more cash to spend on baseball cards, we founded Roberts, Roberts, and Tye, a lawn mowing business. We used Chuck's Dad's push mower because Dad wouldn't let us anywhere near his power machine. One amputation in the family was enough! For $1.50 we'd mow and rake the lawn and divide the fee three ways. Lucky was our fourth partner, but he wasn't part of the split. After all, he just found a shady spot and lay there sleeping in the grass while we worked. Lucky was dubbed Tripod and became the mascot of the neighborhood. Lucky had balls of tempered steel, but few teeth and a 25% deficiency in the leg department, which was not a formula for success. He couldn't avoid a dog fight. We and our friends were very protective of him and did our best to prevent these because we knew what the outcome would be. Lucky never had a chance. His lifetime record was 0-11. On day, up at Chuck Tye's house, a mean 70 lb. boxer started after Lucky, who at that point weighed maybe 30 lbs, much of that fat. Johnny Buffa, who was painting the house next door, came running and dumped a whole gallon of Cook's white house paint on the boxer which quelled his tendency to homicide. Mom frequently had to take Lucky to the vet to get him stitched up. No matter how big the dog, and how great his weight disadvantage, German Shepherds, Boxers, Pit Bulls, he was always ready to go, a willing, eager participant. We'd have to attack his adversaries with coke bottles, ball bats, whatever was at hand to save Lucky's life,

and all the neighborhood guys would always jump right in. However, Lucky was afraid of two four legged creatures - Denver's big shaggy gray tom cat, Stinker, who was named for his disposition, and Mrs. Marchio's five pound Chihuahua, Pancho. Lucky would walk clear across the street to avoid Pancho as he snarled and yipped vigorously to protect his turf.

One day, we were up at the vacant lot in the midst of a heated contest. An elderly lady whose name I can't recall, owned a really big and mean German Shepherd. Her house was adjacent to the vacant lot and she kept the snarling monster safely locked behind a chain-link fence. He barked, growled and bared his teeth anytime anyone even thought about coming near him. We called this nasty beast "Butthole". It was my turn to bat and I stepped up to the plate.

Dutch was pitching. He got a couple by me, but swinging with bad intentions, I nailed the third one, a line drive into the weed patch that was right field. As I rounded first, digging for second, Butthole scrambled over the fence and came after me. Witnesses swore that Lucky, seeing me in danger, sprinted as fast as his three legs could carry him, dived and got Butthole by the back leg. Needless to say, this was not a fight Lucky was destined to win. Butthole soon had Lucky on his back and was biting Lucky's throat. Terry, who was always fearless, grabbed the Louisville Slugger and raced toward the jaws of death. Getting there just in time, he swung mightily, nailing Butthole right square in the ass. Butthole, having won the match easily, looked at Terry who had murder in his eye as he cranked up for a second shot and decided to beat a hasty, well advised retreat, yelping in pain. Like I said, we were "The Three Musketeers, and it was one for all and all for one. Once again, we bundled Lucky up and made the trip to the pet hospital where Lucky received over twenty stitches.

When I was nine, always knowing that I would be a musician, I began to study the violin. It was simply time to start. As I practiced every night, Lucky would begin to howl, "woo, woo," like a wolf. Dad said it was because dogs have better hearing than humans and the high frequencies were hurting his ears. I strongly disagreed. I often heard Lucky's cries of pain as a result of him tweaking the wire in his jaw. If he chomped down just right, something misfired and he would yelp in discomfort for a few seconds. His howls were not the same thing. I was, and am, convinced that he was singing. He would sit right beside the window where I was practicing and join in. It made perfect sense that my dog would be a music lover.

Lucky, much like Terry and me, could not abide dogmatic authority figures. It was his front yard and just because you had a uniform on didn't mean that you could walk right up as if it were yours. Mailmen, gas company meter readers, milkmen, it was always the same. He would bark and snarl, doing his best to convince you he was a canine Al Capone. I assured the trespassers that, since Lucky had very few teeth, they were in no immediate danger. Then one day the mailman kicked Lucky in his bad jaw and he cried out in pain. Terry, who was maybe 12 at the time saw this happen, ran out and confronted the mailman, yelling "Hey motherfucker - you kick my dog again and they'll be scraping your sorry ass off the god damn street." Then for emphasis he tried to get right in the mailman's face but had to settle for putting the evil eye on the man's solar plexus. Terry always had a flare for the dramatic and a vocabulary that was very advanced for his age. (He hung out with Uncle Clarence, who having been a sailor for nine years, cussed like one.) Terry was always inordinately strong, and in his youth, more than a little nuts. (Terry and Lucky were a lot alike, very bellicose!) If the mailman had pressed the point, Terry might have just pulled it off. Then the post office called and told us that if we didn't put Lucky in during mail delivery time, they would no longer deliver our mail. I was confused by all this consternation over an overweight, three legged cocker spaniel with no teeth. Didn't adults have anything better to do? We had no choice. Each day about a half hour before delivery time. We'd round up Lucky and put him in the basement.

As Lucky got on in years, always of a good appetite, he really began to put on the weight. In fact he became quite obese. Then one day he collapsed in the back yard and appeared to be having difficulty breathing. We rushed him to the pet hospital and the vet said Lucky had had a mild heart attack. Then he really took us to task over Lucky's weight saying we were over feeding him and this was going to kill him. Terry and I fed Lucky and what he got was just what a dog of his breed and size was supposed to have, a half can of Strongheart in the morning and the other half in the evening. (All the healthy pet foods didn't exist in those days.) He also got a few table scraps, but certainly nothing sufficient to cause his level of obesity. The Doc assured us that Lucky was getting much more food from somewhere. After we brought him home, Terry and I followed him after breakfast, one day. First he went to Mrs. Cannon's house, climbed the steps up her back porch and began to whine pitifully. Feeling sorry for him, Mrs. Cannon gave him a bowl of table scraps. After this he sauntered over to Mrs. Fisher's house and repeated his performance with the same result. Then it was on to Mrs. Burkett's. Nearly everyone on the block was feeding him! He would sit up, dangle his one front leg and whine, a pathetic sight, till he got what he wanted! I finally had to go around and tell people that he had to lose weight and to please stop feeding him, that they were going to kill him. I assured them that no matter how pitiful he looked, he was a canine hustler. We fed him what he was supposed to have and that his weight should have made this obvious. The answers were always the same - "But he's so cute!" My efforts were successful and Lucky lost a lot of weight.

As we matured, we stopped playing baseball at the vacant lot. It was no longer a vacant anyway. One day a crew had shown up, unloaded a bulldozer off a truck and began digging the hole that would be the basement of the new house where Richard Higgins would live.

Time marches on. With high school activities and having realized the intrinsic worth of high school girls, Terry and I no longer had time to spend with Lucky like in the old days. He didn't care. He was getting old and hadn't the energy of his youth. He was happy to have a pat on the head, his half can of Strongheart and a blanket to lie on where he napped everyday. He lived for 17 years which was really amazing when you took into account all the misfortunes he experienced.

When Lucky passed, I was well into adulthood, married and working as a social worker.

If, back then, we had had the same standards for pet care that we have today, fenced in yards, leash laws, healthy pet food, Lucky would have had a much easier life. Most of our neighbors were more concerned about paying the light bill or having enough for groceries.

But then Lucky would have been deprived of the pleasure of going where he wanted, whenever he wanted to go, and the opportunity to show the world how brave he was. He was one hell of a dog!

JULY 1956

Terry and Lucky

Chapter 6 "Mom versus Ted Williams"

I had as good a mom as a fellow can have. She grew up fast. Poor people do because they have to. She was an Oklahoma farm girl, a depression kid who knew, first hand, what it feels like not to have enough to eat. She dropped out of school as a freshman to go to work because her family needed the money. She met Clifford Elmer Roberts and got married at 17, had me when she was 18 and Terry when she was 19. She couldn't even vote and she already had two kids. Mom was nurturing, industrious (she always had a job and worked till she was over 70) and very brave. Nobody ever messed with her kids.

Once, this bully, Billy Joe, was picking on my brother. Terry could have taken him in the first round, but then he'd have had to deal with Billy Joe's five older brothers. Not even Terry was that nuts. Mom came out with fire in her eyes and told Billy Joe what was what. Billy Joe cussed Mom out. Mom called him a "filthy talking human" then said she ought to "tan his hide". Billy Joe must have realized that Mom meant business and would do what ever she had to even if it involved all five of his brothers. Realizing how silly he'd look getting his butt kicked by a woman, Billy Joe came to his senses. Mom wouldn't really have hit him, but he didn't know that.

Our family all really loved baseball. It started when I was 6 and Terry 5 when Dad brought home a softball and bat and began teaching us the fundamentals in the back yard. At first, he gave us five strikes because we needed them. Then we went to Montgomery Ward's and got a couple of cheap infielder's gloves and we were on our way. Right away, Terry was a much better fielder, but I was the better hitter. We started listening to "Play by play with Larry Ray", the radio broadcast of the Kansas City Blues games with Dad telling us what was going on. The Blues were the Yankees American Association farm club, and we had all their greats before they became stars: Mickey Mantle, Phil Rizzuto, Hank Bauer, Yogi Berra. My favorite player was Bill "Moose" Skowron. I liked him so much I became a first baseman. We'd go out to the old Municipal Stadium and watch our boys play every chance we got. I saw Mickey Mantle's last minor league game. It was a double header with the old AAA Milwaukee Brewers, our arch-rivals. Mickey hit four homers in the first game and two more in the second, and before he even got to the dugout from the 6th homer, the call came for him to catch the first train to New York. Mickey never looked back.

In 1955, Kansas City got a major league team when the Philadelphia Athletics were purchased by Arnold Johnson and he moved them here. They added an upper deck to the already obsolete Municipal Stadium at 22nd and Brooklyn to accommodate the larger crowds. We were ecstatic. The A's weren't very good, but for the price of a ticket, we could see all the American League greats, Whitey Ford, Al Kaline and Ted Williams. Terry and I got a buck apiece for passing out handbills once a week, advertising discount specials for a neighborhood dry cleaners. As soon as we heard the A's were coming we started saving every cent we made for tickets, except what we spent on Topp's and Bowman's baseball cards. The necessity to stretch your money and look for bargains to make ends meet had been drummed in to us by our always practical Mom. My brother got a season schedule and we concentrated on double headers where you got two games for the price of one. Double headers with the Yankees and Red Sox sold out quickly because everyone wanted to see the reigning American League stars, Mickey Mantle and Ted Williams. Terry managed to get double header tickets for both teams. We were elated! Time dragged by like a sedated snail as we waited anxiously for the big day.

Finally the big day came. We were going to see the mighty Red Sox. Mom made a thermos of Cherry Kool-Aid and wonderful ham sandwiches with Gulden's mustard and bread and butter pickles on Roma Bakery Italian bread. She threw in a pack of Hostess Sno-Balls,

Marshmallow and coconut covered chocolate cupcakes, for each of us, and packed our lunches

in a brown paper sack. We were saving our food money for an after game dinner at Arthur Bryant's Barbecue. (Calvin Trillin, renowned food critic, called Bryant's beef brisket the best food he's ever eaten in his book American Fried. Bryant's was at 18th and Brooklyn, just four blocks from the ballpark. They featured massive beef sandwiches with Arthur's unique sauce. It was quite thick, tasting of red peppers and vinegar and packed a serious wallop. (I bought a bottle before Arthur died and my wife wouldn't let me put it in the refrigerator. She feared it would eat its way through the plastic container, take out the bottom of the appliance, and work its way all the way through to China!) Bryant's also had incredible French fries, fried crispy brown and dripping with grease - the kind of food that moved in and took up permanent residence in your veins. But what a way to go. Arthur's dog, a champion brown and white boxer with a red bow tied around his neck, lay with his head resting on his paws, in the corner. This was against health department regulations, but I suspect someone at City Hall had a jones for barbecue. The customers would wait in line as Richard, Arthur's nephew, sliced the meat and built your sandwich with his bare hands.

Mom drove us to the ball park early so we could watch batting practice. We walked over to the ramp that led from the Red Sox clubhouse to the field and joined a group of enthusiastic boys there. Ted Williams, called “The Splendid Splinter” because of his lean, lanky frame, emerged from the tunnel like a deity, with much bravado, a smug smile on his rugged, sun tanned face. He paused and surveyed his kingdom like a feudal lord watching over his serfs. Then he strolled, apart from the other players, right by us. Terry was an avid autograph collector. (He still has them all.) We extended our autograph books with pens pleading, “Please, Mr. Williams”.

“Catch me between games, boys”, he muttered as he kept walking.

We watched him blast about every other pitch out of the ball park during batting practice, then found our seats, high up in the General Admission section. The first game went by quickly and the Red Sox won, of course. We went back to the ramp by the visiting team clubhouse to be ready for Williams as he came in for a fresh uniform and some refreshments before the second game, hoping he make good on his promise to sign our books.

“Please, Mr. Williams, you promised.” We reminded him of his earlier statement as we held our books over the rail. “Catch me after the game, boys” he grumbled and walked by without even looking at us and disappeared into the clubhouse.

We were young and trusting. We were also confused and disappointed. In our world, if you made a commitment, you kept it. We ate our lunches and hoped the A's would do better in game two. The second game started. As was our practice, we scouted around for empty box seats. We found two choice seats along the third base line and moved to the much better spot to view the second contest. The A's pitching in those days wasn't much, except for Alex Kellner, and Alex wasn't on the mound that day. We finished the other half of the Kool-Aid and the Sno-Balls we'd saved to get us through game two. The A's were soon way behind, so at the beginning of the ninth inning, following Williams' instructions, we returned to the ramp leading to the visiting team clubhouse to be ready for him. If the A's mounted an amazing comeback, which was highly improbable, we could watch it from there. But, as usual, the A's went down, not with a bang but a whimper. The Red Sox strolled by, one by one, and finally we saw Ted Williams approaching with his lazy, haughty saunter. Once again we enthusiastically extended our autograph books and pens. We were not easily discouraged. Then Williams stopped for a moment.

"Hey, Mr. Williams, you said after the game."

"Meet me outside the clubhouse, boys," was his terse reply.

He walked off leaving 15 or 20 hugely disappointed kids. We asked an usher where the clubhouse was, then looked for Mom to let her know where we would be. We found her radiant coral and gray '55 Chevy convertible easily. (Dad sold cars at Bill Allen Chevrolet in North Kansas City and we got a special discount that General Motors gave their sales staff. Dad could buy a new car so cheap he could sell it at the end of the year for more than he had paid for it, so Mom always had the latest top model.) Who could miss a coral and gray convertible? Mom was always right where she said she would be when she said she would be there! There was no middle ground with Terry. When he wanted something, he just had to have it, and he usually got it, and he wanted Williams' autograph! He told Mom to hang on while we waited for him outside the clubhouse. She said okay, and that she would find a place to park and join us.

We found the clubhouse and waited nervously. Ten minutes, fifteen minutes went by and still no Williams. Mom walked down the sidewalk with a rare impatient look on her face. She found it dumbfounding that Williams wouldn't sign autographs on the field, and thought we should leave. Terry pleaded with Mom for just a few more minutes.

A taxi pulled up and two very attractive young ladies got out.

They were wearing party clothes. One was a slim bleached blonde and the other a statuesque brunette. Mom grimaced and looked at them suspiciously. I was only 13 and didn't know it then, but have since come to realize these women were hookers. Mom had the situation pegged, eyed the women with disdain and said, "Come on, boys, let's go!" But Terry, who had the Slankard stubborn streak in him, would not budge. Twenty, then thirty minutes went by and Mom uncrossed her arms and looked at her watch.

Finally, the Splendid Splinter made his regal appearance, radiant in an expensive suit and tie, flashed the girls a big warm smile, put an arm around each girl's waist, ignored us, and walked off.

Now Mom looked down on profanity of any sort and hardly ever swore, but she caught up with Williams and let him have a full salvo. "You son-of-bitch! You told these kids to wait here and they did for thirty-five minutes. Now you owe them an autograph."

Williams walked on pretending my mother didn't exist in the exalted, pampered, privileged world of a $100,000 a year athlete.

"These kid's ticket money pays your salary, you jerk", Mom roared. "Can't your floozies wait thirty seconds?"

Williams didn't give a darn. It was obvious he felt he owed the fans nothing. I lost all respect for him for all time that day. The fact that thousands of working people scrimped to afford the tickets that bankrolled his lifestyle either hadn't occurred to him or he didn't care. I know from personal experience that Micky Mantle, who had more power, was faster, and anchored his team to six world championships (Williams had none), would stand around signing autographs till all the kids went home. Williams didn't have to sign autographs, I guess, but he sure didn't have the right to lead us kids on for five hours at a time. He could have been honest and told us he just wasn't signing autographs that day. We adjourned to Bryant's, but I was so angry I could hardly eat my barbecue and greasy fries.

Later that summer, the A's had autograph day, where the players from both teams were required to line up on the field and sign the fan's books after the game. My brother joined the queue and got Ted Williams signature. Being mostly German, I can hold a grudge forever! I got the players on either side of Williams' to sign, then looked at him and said, "Hey, man, I don't want your autograph", and walked off.

A few years later, Williams hit his 500th homer while in Kansas City. As he rounded second base in his famous trot, he raised his defiant head and spit, blowing a huge lugey at the fans and press box in the ultimate act of contempt. In our neighborhood, spitting at someone was grounds for a broken nose! In subsequent interviews, Williams claimed that he was spitting at the Boston press who had hounded him his whole career. (In that case, why didn't he wait till he got back to Beantown to spit?) Kansas City hadn't even been in the league but a couple of years. Splendid my backside!

My Mom, though she never made the headlines, and couldn't hit a 98 mile per hour fastball 400 feet, was a bigger hero than Ted Williams ever was. She had a ready smile, always treated everyone with respect, and absolutely came through for those of us who were counting on her.

Others may place laurels at Williams' feet, but I remember him spitting at the fans, deliberately deceiving us, and Mom giving him what for.

AUG 1955

First Base, Ron Roberts (Left)

Short Stop, Terry Roberts (Right)

Chapter 7 "Campy"

The misconception that the 50's were some "Leave it to Beaver" halcyon were advanced by people with absolute tunnel vision. Segregation was unconditional and prejudice was ubiquitous. The Northeast area in the fifties was a real melting pot, a microcosm of Americana, Italians, Irish, Swedes, Mexicans, Germans, with one glaring exception. Because of aforementioned mafia edicts, there were absolutely no African-Americans. We lived in a real cocoon. If you never left the Northeast area, you wouldn't have known that black people existed. The first real progress in race relations came in the music business, when in 1938, Benny Goodman, a Jew, introduced his new quartet which featured Benny on clarinet, Gene Krupa who was Polish, on drums, Teddy Wilson on piano and Lionel Hampton on vibes, both African-Americans, completed the ensemble. The black and white split was right down the middle. Progress was dormant for another 10 years till baseball, in the form of Branch Rickey, signed Jackie Robinson to play second base for the Brooklyn Dodgers, which created a real furor. But Rickey and Robinson had made their decision with great resolve. At one point Robinson received death threats, and the Dodgers, who had already seen Jackie's worth as a man and an athlete, voted unanimously to all wear number 42, so that any long range assassin would be confused as to which Dodger to shoot.

A trickle of great black baseball players made their way to the Major Leagues, including the great Satchel Paige, who was by then, well past his prime, but still a force, Don Newcomb, Larry Doby, and one of my all-time favorites, catcher Roy Campanella, who joined Jackie with the Dodgers.

There were no rock stars in 1952. That social phenomenon had yet to occur. Baseball ruled and all our heroes made their living on the diamond. Idols were Mickey Mantle, Ted Williams, or Duke Snider - not basketball or football players or some strutting high heeled effete guitarist with face paint. The most desired possessions were a Wilson or Rawlings fielder's mitt, or a Louisville Slugger bat and not a Gibson Les Paul guitar. The big singers were Frank Sinatra and Tony Bennett, Italians. Later it was Dion DiMucci and the Belmonts.

I wasn't confined to the all white existence that was Northeast, however. Every Sunday, Mom, Terry and I, , walked up to St. John Avenue and caught the Northeast bus to First Presbyterian Church at 10th St. and Tracy (It burned down many years ago). It was there that I had my first experience with the repugnance of racism. The first African-American I knew was the affable Charles, who was the one armed church custodian. During the summer of 1951, the minister decided that

Vacation Bible School attendance wasn't what it should be, so he hired a bagpiper in full kilt to walk through the neighborhood, like the pied piper, inviting black kids to participate. He got a few takers and that was where I met Roy, who was a great kid and a terrific softball player. At 9, I wasn't quite ready to challenge the judgment of adults, but later foment was born right there! The congregation was unanimous in their fury and they demanded the minister's resignation. Vacation Bible School only lasted two weeks and the debacle soon blew over. The Church, instead of leading the fight for social justice, stood, flaccid, on the sidelines.

Because the Kansas City Blues were a farm club for the Yankees, all the guys I played ball with were Yankee fans. The fact that two of the big stars, Yogi Berra and Phil Rizzuto were Italian, was even better. And they all hated the Dodgers because they had five black players, Jackie Robinson, Junior Gilliam, Joe Black, Don Newcomb and the great Hall of Fame catcher,

Roy Campanella. I really liked Roy, but any discussion of catchers was usually quashed with the declaration that Yogi was better than Roy and Yogi's supporters were numerous, adamant and quite prepared to back up their opinion with a well aimed fist-burger! I kept my views to myself. Terry and I laughed at Campanella's Gillette adjustable razor commercial. Roy lathered up, and took a stroke and pronounced "Mah face is tender", which cracked us up. The idea that

this big, tough looking catcher had a tender face seemed contradictory.

A common remark was

that the Dodgers were nothing but a bunch of "fungees". Now I was a Yankee fan like everyone else, but I realized that a great World Series required a worthy opponent. During the regular season, I pulled for the Yanks in the American league and the Dodgers in the National League. But come post season, it was all Yankees. The series **was** the Yankees and the Dodgers! What was a series without Mantle, Berra, Phil Rizzuto and Allie Reynolds versus Duke Snider, Gil Hodges, Don Newcomb and Campy, blasting homers, blocking home plate or throwing out base runners. It would be like heavyweight champ, Rocky Marciano, fighting a middleweight. I pulled for the Yanks, but had great respect for the Dodgers. I was alone in this matter. All my teammates had utter contempt for the Dodgers and their five "fungees". The Yanks always won, but those were some of the best baseball games ever played.

Adding to my confusion was my Dad's stories of having seen Satchel Paige pitch for the Kansas City Monarchs in the old Negro League at Municipal Stadium. Dad told the story of how Satch, in a superb display of confidence and showmanship, sent all his fielders except the catcher, to the dugout, and then proceeded to double-pump his way through three consecutive strikeouts! Dad also claimed to have seen Paige pitch both ends of a double header. Satch was a major league relief pitcher when he was well into his fifties. The dichotomy was about how these men could be so revered and completely marginalized at the same time.

In 1954, I tried out for the Northeast Community Center baseball team at first base. I made the team as a starter, but we were terrible. We lost every game. The worst player on the team was, undoubtedly, "Little Bennie T.", a loud mouth who was half Italian and half Irish. The only time he got to play was when we had only eight other guys show up. Then Sim, the manager, would put Bennie in right field and pray that no one hit one out there.

At the beginning of the season, Bennie made the announcement that he wasn't taking the
field against any Fungees.

The Brown vs. The Topeka Board of Education Supreme Court ruling passed in 1954. Other schools were forced to integrate, but not Northeast. The mafia had more juice than the Court it would seem.

In 1957, Campy slugged his last homer, threw out his last runner and called his last great game. He was behind the wheel of his shiny new Cadillac convertible when a terrible crash occurred. Campy would spend the rest of his life, as a paraplegic in a wheel chair. As undefeatable as ever, he became a spokesperson for the disabled and wrote an autobiography, It's Good To Be Alive that was on the best seller list for nearly a year.

Time flew by and about 1980, I was coming home from a gig. I stopped and picked up a pint of Haagen Daz Cherry-Vanilla ice cream on the way home and settled in in front of the TV hoping to catch a late movie. I was pleasantly surprised to find that the 1974 made-for-television movie, "It's Good To Be Alive", starring Paul Winfield as Campy and Ruby Dee as his wife, was being shown. It depicted Campy's struggle to reach the major leagues. I was very surprised to find that Campy was bi-racial. His father was Italian and his mother African-American. No one had ever wondered why Campy had an Italian surname. By fifties standards, if you were any black, you were all black. I laughed out loud when I remembered "Little Bennie T". This irony exposes the patent stupidity of racism as well as anything I have encountered in my life. Hey Bennie T, who couldn't catch a fly ball in a bushel basket, Campy was every bit as much Italian as you!

Chapter 8 "Mr. Bianco"

Teachers are close to my heart. I was married to one for 14 years. Her wonderful sister, Judy, taught for many years. Having spent the better part of 23 years getting educated, kindergarten through grade 12, and being in and out of college over the next ten years, with several majors, I've had a virtual myriad of them. Most of them were okay, some were good, and some awful. I had an English teacher my sophomore year who showed up, handed out such classics as "My Friend Flicka" and proceeded to put her head down on her desk and sleep off her hangover - and another clown named Babbitt, a pompous, puffed up little man, who spent more time bragging about his naval exploits during World War II than he did teaching Biology. A few were great and they had a profound impact on my life. One of those was Harry J. Bianco, a born teacher! I met him in Orchestra class at the age of 13 as an 8th grade violinist. Saying Harry was energetic wouldn't do him justice. He was perhaps the most optimistic and enthusiastic person I've met in my 70 years.

The first day of school in 1955, I walked into Orchestra class, found a seat, took out my violin and rosined my bow. Mr. B. walked in. He was a young, slender, already balding, bespectacled Italian, the son of immigrants. I had no idea at that time how he would be the catalyst in forming the trajectory of my life.

He had grown up speaking Italian in the home, but had no sign of an ethnic accent. Harry came from Duluth and he had a decided Minnesota twang, a unique accent indeed! That was the first time I had heard the expression, "jeez". He usually wore just a white shirt and tie. He had a suit coat somewhere, but he usually ditched it because it got in his way when he was conducting, something he excelled at - and man, could he ever play the clarinet! I heard him warm up one day on the opening clarinet *glissando* of Gershwin's "Rhapsody In Blue", one of my favorite pieces in my youth, and he became my new hero - better than Mickey Mantle. It was obvious that Mr. B. really knew his stuff. He got right down to business, had us all play, and assigned chairs. I landed in the middle of the violin section.

While having a great love of music, I was becoming disillusioned with the violin.

I have loved listening to classical music all of my life, but it was becoming obvious to me that that was not the music I wanted to play. I viewed orchestral musicians as essential cogs in a beautiful machine who conceded their individuality and creativity to the conductor. That concept was not in my gestalt. I already had ideas of my own and was trying, unsuccessfully, to compose. I had seen the movie, "The Fabulous Dorseys" featuring Jimmy and Tommy Dorsey playing themselves, while in the 7th grade. As youths, they had gotten in trouble for jazzing up tunes in band class. That was the first time I had seen someone improvise - instant composition! I was immediately struck with how great life as a professional musician would be, traveling around, doing what you loved and getting paid for it. And the big bonus was that they worked at night and didn't have to get up early in the morning, a concept I could endorse. And they played jazz which was beginning to work its mojo on me. I made up my mind right there... This was for me. I started buying records, Duke Ellington, Glen Miller - and I joined the Columbia Record Club and got the likes of Bobby Hackett, Jonah Jones and the great Peggy Lee. I also liked rock 'n roll - Bill Haley and the Comets and "Fats" Dominoe. It had become obvious to me that there wasn't a violin in there anywhere. I had began the violin because of all the great memories of Grandpa, but I had lost interest in western swing about the time I outgrew Gene Autry. The first time I heard Earl Bostic play "Harlem Nocturne" had been a transcendental experience and I begin to lobby for an alto saxophone like Bostic's. Mom and Dad had already bought me a violin and they looked askance at this idea. Saxophones are expensive instruments and one usually had to prove

one's worth on the much less expensive clarinet before matriculating to saxophone. My Dad also didn't much approve of my interest in music as my life's work. He said musicians were all a bunch of drunken bums and that I was too smart for that kind of life, that I should be a lawyer, the profession he had chosen for me before I even started school. This infuriated me, something my dad accomplished frequently. He felt he had a divine right to make everyone's decisions for them. Harry Bianco was a musician. He was also a dedicated family man and a devout Catholic and never, ever a drunken bum. Mom, while not really understanding the thought processes of a creative kid, always tried to help me at whatever I became interested in. She said we should talk to Mr. Bianco about this and see what our options were. I heartily approved this idea. I had already accepted Mr. B. as my mentor and I couldn't have chosen a better man. So Mom made an appointment with the always accommodating Mr. B. to discuss my future. She knew that I had no chance of talking Dad into an expensive saxophone and was looking for a way to enhance my creative growth that didn't entail a large loan. Mr. B.
welcomed us to the band room and we all sat down. I explained how I wanted to play jazz, and never having heard Stephan Grappelli or Joe Venuti, I had no idea what a great jazz instrument violin can be in the

right hands. Mr. B. got right to the heart of the matter and asked me if I really wanted to play saxophone specifically, or did I just want to play jazz? I thought for a moment, then affirmed the latter. It was like baseball. I didn't care where I played as long as I was in the game. Mr. B. was a working professional and knew the scene. He suggested that I take up the string bass, that good bass players were always in short supply and that I had talent, and could, at the very least, work my way through college. I mulled this over and Mr. B.'s logic won out. Mom asked how much this was going to cost and Mr. B. replied, nothing, the right answer. He said between Northeast Jr. and Northeast Sr. he had more basses than he did players and that I could take one home to practice. The die was cast. This was acceptable to Mom and me.

Mom drove us to school every day, but we walked home. I was wondering how I was going to get the student model aluminum bodied bass home. I enlisted my pal, Jim Sander, a fellow musician, who would become my brother-in-law, to help. He took the spike and I took the neck and we lugged it the 13 blocks to my house.

Harry was a reed man. He showed me how he thought I should hold the bass, told me the letters of the bass clef staff, and gave me the bass folder with the music of the Northeast Jr. High Orchestra, and I was on my own. I started practicing at home, concentrating on the repertoire the orchestra was playing. The bass parts were simpler than the lines I'd been playing on violin and it didn't take long. I was a bassist, bass man, bass player, whatever moniker you prefer. I also started learning the bass lines to popular rock 'n roll tunes by ear. Jazz was beyond me at that point, but I was listening and learning. Mr. B. encouraged me, telling me what a good job I'd been doing, then after about 60 days, he promoted me to first chair, over the other fellow who played bass. I worked hard and Mr. B. let me keep the bass over the summer.

The fall of 1956, my sophomore year, was a big one for me. I had grown over six inches in the past year and I was now at the Northeast Senior High School building. The orchestra was much better. I was now playing with some kids that were 17 years old and much more advanced players. Then Harry made my year. He invited me to be the bassist in "The Blue Notes", the stage band. He said I had done a good job and he was sure I was ready. I will never forget the first rehearsal. We actually had an arrangement of "Sophisticated Lady", a Duke Ellington tune. Mr. B. loved Ellington. I believed then, and still adhere to the conviction that Edward Kennedy "Duke" Ellington is our greatest American composer. African/American musicians had no place in classical music in those days. The orchestras embraced Gershwin, who was Jewish and white, but Ellington was ignored. African/American melodies and rhythms were okay for the concert stage if they were written and orchestrated by white men like Gershwin and Ferde Groffe. The brilliant "Porgy and Bess" was huge, but "The Black, Brown and Tan Fantasy" was overlooked. But black or white, I didn't care, Duke was my man and I was playing his music, thanks to Mr. B. We were short handed in the sax section, so Mr. B. frequently filled in on baritone. Our level of performance increased exponentially when this happened. At 15, I was living my dream! Then Mr. B. introduced me to Everett Green, who was older than me and a trombonist in the orchestra and stage band. He said Everett also played piano and liked jazz and the two of us had a lot in common. I started getting to orchestra early and working out with Everett before orchestra began. Then Everett asked me to audition for "The Krackerjacks", a rock 'n roll band he was playing in. I copped the gig and turned pro, working my first professional engagement, a private party, at the "Kopper Kettle" restaurant in Raytown. I got $4 for a 3 hour engagement and had huge blisters on my fingers, but I didn't care. It was a small price to pay. I was a pro. I took my four bucks and bought a Stan Kenton album, "Adventures in Rhythm", at Sears. My Dad thought I was wasting my money on all those damned records. In less then a year and a half from the time Mr. B. told me what he thought I should do, it all came to fruition. He couldn't have given me better advice. The bass became my life, creatively and professionally. I was merely putting in my time from then on as a high school student. I had found my place in the world, the night life would be my life! I got above average grades, enough to keep my Dad off my back, but the administration had me identified as an underachiever. They said my performance wasn't consistent with what someone of my intelligence should be doing. I told them that I had gotten straight E's (A's in those days) in every music class, had gone from a beginner to a working professional and made second chair in the "All City Orchestra" in less than a year and a half, without having the benefit of a single lesson on bass viol. Then I dismissed what I perceived as nonsense with "underachiever my ass", and walked out. This got me a conference with the

principal, the counselor and my Dad. They spouted a bunch of professional motivational jargon

that got them nowhere. I pointed out that my Dad was a high school dropout and making more money then any of them, which got me some points with Dad, but not the administration. I told them I was bored with high school and couldn't wait to get out and that since I was well on my way to graduation, the point of the thing, I couldn't see any reason to continue the discussion. That ended it. I never suffered from a lack of confidence, and was sick of other people making my decisions for me, and I was declaring my independence. Apparently, the principal had talked with Harry about me, because Harry then took me aside and told me that a well rounded education was very important and I should never lose sight of that, that knowledge was an end of and unto itself. From him I could accept this, and I tried a little harder, but I really just wanted to be gone and get on with my life. Harry put his hand on my shoulder and told me that I was like a lot of bright kids, that I thought I knew more than I actually did. Harry was right, he always was. What he understood was that none of the other teachers or counselors (except my English teacher, Cosette Davis) knew how to relate to a really creative young man who was just trying to find his way in a very stifling, regimented environment.

I played every job the Krackerjacks got, which wasn't too many because we weren't very good. In the meantime, I decided to expand my musical horizons. I was working 18 hours a week at Agron's Market and I took my earnings and bought a Harmony full bodied arch top electric guitar from Van De Weghe Music on Independence Avenue and Van Brunt. My Dad nearly broke a string! He yelled at me about how foolish

I was with my money. I countered with the fact that the germane point was that it was **my** money. I was appalled at his hypocrisy. He had a basement full of expensive fishing tackle, 3 of everything, while Mom worked 40 hours a week to pay off our seriously in-the-arrears grocery bill. Like my brother said, "The only thing I ever learned from Dad was what not to do!" That's why Mr. Bianco was so important to me. I wasn't getting any kind of help from Dad.

I soon tired of the Krackerjacks, who were saddled with the leader's son as singer and guitarist. He could do neither. At 16, I decided to step out on my own and start my own band. The "Satellites" were born. I recruited Terry to play piano. He was okay as long as I wrote out every note he played. He was a good reader, but could do nothing without the music in front of him. I wrote out "Fats" Domino lines for him that I had picked off records. I had an acquaintance, Phil Harris, who played an adequate tenor sax. My Dad's bosses' son, Larry Patterson, played guitar and sang, and he recruited his friend, Johnny Greenlease who was a 13 year old whiz on the drums. Larry and I split the vocals and I played lead guitar and bass. We covered some Elvis, Ricky Nelson, Fats Domino, Carl Perkins and Duane Eddy, with me on "twangy guitar". The guitar I had bought and taught myself how to play, that Dad had raised so much hell about, had already paid for itself.

The aluminum bass I was using had originally been painted with a *faux* wood finish, but a couple of decades of students had left it dented and with many chips in the paint. My Dad was the lease manager at Kelley-Williams Ford. Since the bosses son was in the band I had an idea. I asked Harry, that since the bass looked so bad, was it okay if we had it painted and the dents repaired? The always accommodating Harry said "sure'. Dad's boss gave the go ahead for a freebee and my bass checked into the body and fender shop. They fixed the dents, painted the neck a cream color and painted the body '57 Ford metallic bronze. I had the only two-tone bass with a hot rod paint job in town. The Satellites worked some jobs and actually made the Kansas City Star in an article about local rock 'n roll bands in 1959.

My music career had to take a hiatus in my senior year. I bought the car that Dad had picked out for me (it was my money, but I had no say in the matter), a powder blue

and white four door '54 Chevrolet, an old ladies' car. I took a 24 hour a week job at the Forum

Cafeteria to support my ride, which was a money pit. I didn't get out of there till 9 PM and my

days off were Monday and Tuesday which not only stopped my music career but also killed my social life in one stroke. Something was always wrong with the car and it pretty much kept me broke. So much for Dad's automotive judgment!

After I graduated, I no longer had an instrument. Northeast High School owned

and took back my bass with the hot rod paint job. I did what my Dad wanted me to do and became a history and government major at Kansas City Junior College. I was biding my time. Then in 1961, I got my shot. A drummer named Dick Bragg was looking for a bass player and my friend, Karen Jones, told him about me. He called and I told him that I didn't have a bass. He told me that there was one at Cole Music that I could borrow, and I was on my way. I was playing dances in every small town in Missouri with the Addie Weber Sextet. Mr. Bianco had been right. Bands were always hard up for bass players.

I graduated from K.C.J.C in 1962 and enrolled at Kansas City University, a private college that became a state institution, the University of Missouri at Kansas City the next year. That summer, the only job I could find was as an ice cream man. One day on my route, I ran into my old friend Everett Green. He bought a malt crunch bomb and told me that he was starting a new band and he needed a bass man. That was the opportunity I'd been waiting for, and realizing that I really needed my own instrument, I borrowed $175 from my Grandma and bought my own bass, a Kay, at the Jenkins Music Company. We made some money and I paid Grandma back quickly. Every cent I made from music went straight to Grandma. Then disaster struck. We worked a week at The Seven Keys Country Club, and the drunk that owned it refused to pay us. He said he was broke and we could sue him but it wouldn't do any good, since he didn't have any money. Everett called Mr. Bianco and he told us that there wasn't much we could do, that if we were really serious about music, we should join the musician's union - they took care of

situations like that. Another loan from Grandma made me a member of The American

53

Federation of Musicians, Local 34-1812. Everett's band was getting some work, but not enough for me. The union had this thing called the "call list" and if you were bereft of an engagement for a weekend, you put your name on the list and if a band came up short, they called the list to see who was available to fill their need. I really wasn't all that good, but Mr. B. couldn't have analyzed the situation any better. If you had a pulse and a bass, you got work. I had a good ear and an exceptional memory so I did okay. I picked up a lot of work and was expanding my contacts. I also met a folk singer named Bill Brown and started working with him. It was the folk music heyday and he had lots of jobs for good money. I was where I wanted to be so, in 1964, as a second semester senior, I dropped out of college for the first time. I was saved from my Dad's wrath by geography. He was in New York setting up a leasing division for National Car Rental. So all he could do was yell at me on the phone. While on the road, I realized that I couldn't see my life without my long time girlfriend, Margaret, so I proposed. And to my great good fortune, she accepted. Thinking that a married man needed a real job, I became a Caseworker II at Jackson County Welfare. I lasted a year and a half and that was the only 9 to 5, 40 hour a week day job I had in my whole life. I absolutely hated the regimentation and the early hours. I also continued to play. I was gaining confidence, so one day I called Margaret and told her I wanted to quit and go to the Conservatory. I explained that if music was going to be my life, there was a lot that I needed to learn. I also pointed out that I had been earning extra money with my own band, "The Ron Roberts Quartet" and that I planned to get a part time guitar teaching job. She agreed that this was a good strategy so I resigned and became, once again, a free man. To say that I was the free lance type would be miles short of the mark. It worked out well. I learned a lot and really improved. I also got a six night a week job at the Grecian Gardens restaurant with the terrific accordionist, Don Lipovac.

After a year, "like a bolt out of the blue, fate stepped in and saw me through!" I was asked to join the "Kay Dennis Show", the biggest thing in town. Overnight, I went from an obscure musician to a near celebrity, signing autographs at grocery stores. We did TV specials, commercial jungles which I wrote, and traveled all over the country including work on Broadway in New York and Sunset Boulevard in Hollywood. Shortly after our first TV special, we were completing our contract at he Colony Steakhouse, before we moved on to bigger, better and more lucrative things. I looked out at the audience during "Night and Day" one of my favorite tunes, and there, with a smile a half mile wide, was Harry! He had seen me on TV. At break time I tore off my bass, ran out into the audience and gave him a big hug. I thanked him profusely and assured him that I wouldn't be here if not for him. The always modest Harry, said that I was where I was meant to be and I would have just found another way to get there. I'm not sure that that was the case. But he, if nothing else, he sure sped up the process.

Through the years, on anniversaries or special occasions, Harry always found where I was playing and made that the site of his celebration. Harry wasn't one to hang out in night clubs.

Years later, I successfully ran for a union office and there was

Harry. As always backing me up.

Many years hence, I got a call from Harry. I owned a recording business and Harry had founded “The Fatima Choir”, a Latin mixed chorus. He was going to do an album of Christmas music with them and he wanted me to record it. We ended up doing three. Harry and I were working together, once again. I had a grand time, moving my gear from Catholic Church to Catholic Church to discern which one had the best acoustics. Harry sang tenor and time hadn’t dimmed his enthusiasm for conducting one notch. Harry’s dial went up to 11! It was during this time, while mixing down, that I finally got a chance to tell Harry how much he had meant to me.

He was so modest he reminded me of Tom Mix, “Aw shucks, it was nothing.” Later, I met

Harry’s daughter, Susie, at a birthday party for a friend. I told her how Harry had given me advice that had shaped my life and how much he had meant to me.

When Harry died, I, of course, attended his funeral. I stood in line with a bad knee for 45 minutes. It was obvious that Harry had helped mold more lives than just mine. But that is the stuff great teachers are made of - they help you see the possibilities. When I finally got a chance to express my condolences and gratitude for all that Harry had done for me, his wife, Mary, said that Harry had talked about me all the time. Then Susie said her son had tried several different instruments and was having trouble finding his musical identity. Susie said she told her son that Grandpa had told Ron Roberts to play bass, that that was where the opportunity was and that her son was now studying bass. That nearly floored me. Harry was guiding his grandson through me.

I wrote a piece for the Northeast Alumnae Association newsletter about Harry. But I only recently realized what I would really have liked to have said to him…

"Hey, man, you were in every note I ever played and in every piece I wrote."

Me, 1959

RESPLENDENT IN YELLOW, GREEN, RED AND BLUE jackets, the Satell'
many teen-age bands in the area, practice once a week at the drummer's
on't have to cart the drums around. At the piano is Terry Roberts,
enue, and the drummer is John Greenlease, 1020 West Sixty-third
o right) are Larry Patterson, 431 West Fifty-eighth street terrace;
adstone boulevard, and Ron Roberts, Terry's brother.

The Satellites

Chapter 9 "Uncle Clarence"

Clarence William Slankard, my Mom's kid brother, should have been a bird. He was born to fly. Only 8 years older than me, he was more like my big brother. Clarence's other passion was automobiles. After my Dad got out of the army in 1946, he got a job as a bus driver and we got out first house at 2501 Bellfountain. It stood on a steep terrace with many stairs in the front and also in the back. It was a three generation arrangement, not uncommon in those days, with Grandma, Grandpa, Uncles Wes and Clarence, Mom, Dad, Terry and me. Clarence would take Terry and me and we'd sit on the top step of the back concrete stairway as he taught us how to tell the makes and models of cars from each other. I was the only 4 year old on the block who knew what features distinguished a '40 Ford from the '41 model. Grandpa had his fatal accident not too long after that and we moved to 211 South Monroe. Wes joined the Navy and got married so now we were a family of six.

Clarence, while being rather bright, absolutely hated school. Academe was an anathema to him, like alcohol to Native Americans - it made him crazy. Rough around the edges, he was a worn pair of brown wing tips at the Senior Prom. The only class he liked was wood shop where he made nifty items like book ends and lamps. He was always good with his hands. His heart was in the air. At 14, Clarence had discovered a little private airport on 40 Highway, just East of Hardesty, which was home to a few Cessnas, Piper Cubs and a Beech Bonanza. He would cut school, walk over to Van Brunt street and hitch-hike over there and hang around trying to mooch a ride with someone going up to get in some hours towards obtaining a pilot's license. He would clean up and run errands for free, trying to suck up to the management. The other thing Clarence hated was having to get up early in the morning. Grandma would yell and yell as Clarence remained comatose. Finally, in desperation, she would resort to mild violence - get a glass of water and throw it in Clarence's face which usually did the trick. Then Clarence would go into his morning riff about how his legs hurt too bad to go to school. At 14, he claimed to have developed rheumatism. If Grandma would acquiesce, immediately after she would leave for work selling hot nuts at the downtown T. G. & Y., Clarence would, through some divine intervention no doubt, experience a miraculous recovery and devote the rest of his day to his flying agenda, or work on one of the elaborate model airplanes with balsa wood sticks and tissue paper he was always building.

When Clarence got his report card the shit hit the proverbial fan!

Clarence didn't look like anyone else in the Slankard or Zerbe family. He was of a darker, almond complexion, had slightly crooked teeth, a big nose (like me), a shock of anarchist dark brown hair, a mischievous gleam in his eye and an always present goofy grin. While he was never considered handsome by any standard, Clarence was the sun breaking through at the end of a violent thunderstorm. He just knew in his heart that everything would turn out all right and could convince you of that. He got a job as a delivery boy at a drug store, delivering prescriptions. The money, which would be applied to flying lessons, enabled him to overcome his inability to rise early. Living with Clarence was tantamount to having Rodney Dangerfield as a house guest. Clarence was always telling jokes and had a smart-ass one-liner comeback for every occasion, much to the delight of Terry and me. He always had a large arsenal of loony facial contortions that drove Terry and me to near hysteria. He was our goofy uncle! His wise guy cracks weren't always confined to home turf and weren't always appreciated. Sometimes, he had bad timing. Grandma had to go to Northeast High on more than one occasion to confer with the principal, at the principal's behest, over

Clarence's antics.

At 16, Clarence figured he was wasting his time and dropped out of high school. He got a car, a maroon '48 Ford coupe. It was his treasure. He gave it all his attention, always working on it and it ran great, responding to his every whim, like an extension of his body. Clarence always had a way with machines. Terry and I loved to ride with him. A terrific driver, he would take a corner really fast, tires squealing, and Terry and I would slide across the bench seat. A real original, Uncle C. had a very unique vocabulary - he'd yell at offending drivers, "You Hawaiian Jew!", and his favorite curse was "owl shit". Then he got every teenager's dream job, a soda jerk at the Dairy Queen on Admiral Boulevard, just west of Paseo. Not only did he get free ice cream, but the place was loaded with really cute girls. We were always on Mom to run us by the DQ and Clarence would give us a cone *pro bono*. He'd make anything we wanted. The high point of any summer vacation was when Mom would have some business to take care of and leave us with Clarence at the DQ. That was our idea of heaven. I would get Uncle Clarence to make me a huge sundae with cherries and hot fudge, my favorite, yummo!

By then, Clarence was well into what would become a life pattern, partaking of each of the four basic food groups: nicotine, caffeine, fat and sugar. His favorite thing in the world was a sandwich he would make. First he would fry bologna, then melt Velveeta on top, then scoop it onto a slice of Roma Bakery Italian bread that he had put in the frying pan to properly toast it, then top it with another slice of bread, then flip it to get the concoction toasted on both sides.

That sandwich and hamburgers, the greasier the better, made up his diet. It was negative health food. I rarely ever saw Clarence without a Camel dangling from his lip and a gargantuan mug of black coffee in his hand. I never in my life, ever saw Clarence eat a vegetable.

The Roma Bakery was just down the street from the Dairy Queen, so Clarence, always thinking of others, would stop on his way home and bring cannolis, cream puffs, or chocolate éclairs and bread for everyone. Mom said of Clarence's generosity, that he would give you anything he had, but it was a two way street and if he was in a jam, he expected everything you had. In his world, we all took care of each other.

Nothing is forever, and that included the Dairy Queen. While it was an amusing job, it was not airborne. At 18, Clarence followed his older brother and joined the Navy Air Force, hoping to become a fighter pilot. After signing on the dotted line, he was stuck in the Navy and was informed that he couldn't go to flight school because of vision deficiencies. This broke his heart. He also had a real wanderlust and had joined the Navy to see the world. All he saw was every dive and two-bit beer joint in San Diego. They put him in the Shore Patrol, the Navy version of the Military Police and Clarence became a cop, something he heretofore had held in low regard. He spent his week in a Jeep with another sailor till they were radioed to a location of a bar fight, a regular occurrence with both the Marines and Navy stationed in San Diego. Some swabby would yell "What color is shit?" "Marine green" would be the reply - and off they'd go. Clarence and several others of the Shore Patrol would go in and break up the fight and arrest the combatants by whatever means necessary. Local police had no authority over military personnel. They were federal property and the San Diego Police would have to call in the Shore Patrol. The drunken Marines rarely ever went quietly. Clarence and his SP colleagues would usually have to employ their night sticks and saps (a leather covered blackjack device the police use), pounding the inebriated, basic training stoked offenders into submission before slapping the handcuffs on them and loading them into the jeep. While always being a tough fellow, a 6'1", 185 pounder that nobody messed with, he didn't see brawls as his life's work. He absolutely hated it. If you asked him what he did in the Navy, a scowl would engulf his rugged countenance and he'd spit out, "Beat the shit out of drunk fucking jarheads".

The fact that his older brother was flying daily over the Bering Sea as an observer
with binoculars, looking for Russian submarines in a twin engine Lockeed Neptune P2V, something Clarence would have loved, did nothing but fuel more indignation.

Clarence came home on leave that summer, driving a beautiful pale yellow and black '55 Mercury hardtop. He said he and another "gob" were partners in it. He was the usual load of laughs and having him home was like old times. Then he went back to his old job at the Diary Queen. The thirty days came and went, but Clarence didn't return to the Navy. Clarence always had his own peculiar logic and a simplistic view of what was right and wrong, and this didn't include a gray area. There was never anything even remotely subtle about him. (He was that gaudy Hawaiian shirt that you had bought in a moment of weakness, hanging in your closet that you never wore.) Grandma pleaded with him to go back, but he said that the Navy had lied to him about flying and that he was sick of their bullshit. 30 days turned into 60. Finally a Naval authority called Grandma, telling her that Clarence was in big trouble and that the longer he stayed out, the worse it would be. Grandma, a simple farm girl, was scared to death and told them where Clarence was.

They arrested him at the Dairy Queen and he copped 30 days in the brig. Then, amazingly, the Navy recruiter went to work on him, promising him he could go to Ground Control Approach school, (he'd be one of the guys talking airplanes down like commercial Air Traffic Controllers). Figuring this was going to be as close to flying as he would get, to our amazement, he signed up for six more years. This time the Navy kept its word and Clarence became a G.C.A. and at one point was stationed on the U.S.S. Lexington, an aircraft carrier.

During this time Clarence was transferred to the Naval Air Base at Millington Tennessee, where he met and married Aunt Marcelle and started his family. Mom and I went to visit him there and Clarence, who was approaching 30, seemed to be maturing. He was very devoted to his wife and new son Billy. Navy pay being what it was, and always trying to do better for his family, he moonlighted as the manager of a neighborhood movie theater. He always had a lot of energy. (I often wondered how much of that was due to being wired on caffeine.) Ever the great host and tour guide, Clarence showed us nearby Memphis, Beale Street, famous for Blues venues, and Elvis's house, "Graceland". The wrought iron gate with an outline of Elvis playing his guitar was covered with lipstick and "I love you Elvis" was scrawled everywhere. Elvis had been in the Army and Clarence said he had seen Elvis a couple of times while showing Naval big-wigs around. Elvis had even come over and talked to him once, saying "Hey sailor" and waving him over. I was tremendously impressed but Clarence just shrugged it off. He was never enthralled by the rich and famous.

Clarence had been in a passenger car that was involved in a bad collision and, as a result, was subject to severe headaches which made it difficult for him to view the radar screen hours on end. Tired of Navy pay and military discipline, he used this to get out of the navy a year early. He was always bitter over the Navy misleading him about flying and decided it was time to get even. He was entitled to nine years of the G. I. bill education benefits, one for each year he had served. He told them he wanted to be a career airline pilot and for nine years the government paid for his flying lessons and aircraft rentals. The Navy finally made good on its promise. At last Clarence was flying and he became an expert pilot. During this period he made a career decision, figuring his chances of being an airline pilot were remote at best, he settled for the next best thing and became a Continental Trailways bus driver, based in Wichita. He was a pilot that stayed on the ground. He would drive his bus over a million miles without an accident.

He was always renting a single engine plane and flying into Kansas City on his days off. We had moved to the Red Bridge area of

South Kansas City by then and there was a small private airport on Stateline Road where he would land and we would pick him up. The summer of 1963 he made such a trip. He talked me into going flying with him and up we went in a high wing Cessna 170. He even let me take the yoke. Flying is quite easy - taking off and landing is the difficult part. We flew to Emporia, which is about 125 miles west of Kansas City. Clarence
said that we needed to refuel and took the trajectory to land at a little airport. Everything went smoothly till we touched down. I felt a lurch and saw a concerned look on Clarence's face, which, needless to say, scared the hell out of me. The plane swerved as Clarence manned the yoke and carefully applied the brakes bringing it to a twisting, spinning halt. We had blown a tire at the point of touch down. We stepped out and and trekked into the airport office. All the local flight junkies had seen what had just transpired and began slapping Clarence on the back congratulating him on what a fine job he had done. One guy told me, "That feller's one damn fine flier! You guys could have been dead." Like I said, Clarence always had a way with machines. The tiny airdrome didn't have the tire we needed so Clarence had to call Wichita and have one flown in. We had lunch, awful chicken salad sandwiches as I recall, and then Clarence saw a pin-ball machine. A mischievous

gleam filled his eye, like a kid with a sling shot, he lit a Camel, sat his mug of coffee on the glass and put in a nickel. Now I'd been known to beat a pin-ball machine from time to time, but what unfolded before my eyes was truly amazing. Clarence looked like a swivel hipped squirrel on speed, twisting, jumping, smacking the machine with his left hand and talking to it - "Take that beaver fart," with a Camel in his mouth the whole time. It was personal. Every time I tried something like that the machine would flash "tilt" and shut down. But not Clarence. He knew exactly what he could get away with. He soon drew a crowd of astonished onlookers, cheering him on. He ran the machine up to 99 free games and then left them for the kids to play off. Never having sought greatness, he achieved it that day at the airport. That may have been the single greatest game of pin-ball ever played.

Clarence then went over to the cigarette machine to restock on Camels. He put in a quarter, got a pack, and two quarters back in change. A big grin spread across his face and he said, "Let's try this again." The process was completed with the same result. Clarence kept going till the machine was out of Camels, then switched to Winstons which he gave to me. I asked him if maybe we shouldn't tell someone. He laughed and asked, "How many times have you put money in a machine and got nothing?" The answer was plenty. "Today, we get even." Acknowledging that he had a point, I stuffed my pockets full of Winstons as he filled his with quarters. Finally the wheel came and he flew me back to Kansas City and then returned to Wichita.

In 1964, I married my long time sweetheart, Margaret. On our first vacation together, we decided to go to Denver. Clarence had been assigned to a regular Denver to Wichita run. He routinely drove the bus to Denver, stayed at a hotel where Continental Trailways put up their drivers, then returned to Wichita the next day. We called him and he showed us around Denver. Clarence had a way of making strangers feel like old friends, and Margaret liked my goofy Uncle as much as I did.

Clarence antics became legend among bus drivers. My cousin, Bob Zerbe, told me a classic Clarence tale. Bob was also a flier and he was at a small airport in Texas. A guy came up to Bob and said, "Hey Zerbe, ain't you related to that good 'ol boy, Slankard, the bus driver?" Bob affirmed kinship. "That guy should be a comedian. He gets on his bus with a gray old man wig, see, and he has a cane and he can barely walk. Two other drivers all but carried him onto the bus. Then he collapses into the driver's seat and says, 'Thanks, guys, I think I can make it from here'. One guy was so scared, he got off the bus."

One of Clarence's favorites was to wear a long blonde ladies wig under his driver's hat and blow kisses to the truck drivers as they passed, or pull out his false teeth and clack them. Then there was the one with dark glasses and the white cane… Clarence antics made him Wichita's most popular tour bus driver for Continental Trailways Tours, which were primarily senior citizen scenic bus vacations. He went all over the country and cleaned up in tips. His shtick kept the passengers in stitches.

The years flew by, and I never went through Wichita that I didn't stop in and see him. After his 9 year GI bill subsidy ran out, he didn't fly much. By then, he and Marcelle had three kids and he couldn't afford it. But he had held the Navy accountable for its promise and logged many hours among the clouds.

Always trying to do more for his family, Clarence started doing body and fender repair in his garage in his spare time, and developed a local following. (He painted two of my four MGs.) He had always loved old cars and usually had one around. He figured out a way to make it pay. (I bought his '47 Studebaker Starlight Champion Coupe, which ran so well and looked so good, I drove it for a year, then sold it to an Automotive Museum.)

At age 58, Uncle Clarence's old heart had taken all the nicotine, caffeine, fat and sugar it could stand, and while he was having dinner at home with his family one evening, it quit on him for good. I had resigned myself, long ago, to the likelihood that Clarence would not have a long life. I was so glad that the end came at home with his family and not in some lonesome old hotel room. As I stood crying in front of his casket, hiding behind my Ray-Bans, looking at Clarence one last time, I almost expected him to make one of his daffy faces at me. If he could have, he surely would have. That would have been the way he wanted to go out.

Clarence was a man's man who did everything the hard way, the consummate up stream swimmer. Any time I'm feeling down, I recall one of his loony faces and it always cheers me up. Clarence William Slankard only got 58 years, but he was always vibrantly alive, in the moment, they were action packed, and he lived and enjoyed every minute of every day of every goddam one of them.

Terry 15, Uncle Clarence Slankard 24, the author 16.

Chapter 10 "Sal's Barber Shop"

At 13 years of age and starting to Northeast Jr. High, my thoughts had taken a sharp turn toward the opposite sex and I began to think more about my appearance. Hair was a big thing, thanks to Bill Haley with his spit-curl and Pat Boone's pompadour. All the Italian guys had great haircuts, perfectly combed, with their thick black hair shining with a coating of Lucky Tiger or Brylcreme. The predominant haircut was the ubiquitous flat-top, short and flat on the top, some with "fenders" or "ducktails", long hair on the sides, heavily greased and combed straight back, and some were short all over the head. The latter was very popular with jocks. Some of the devotees of ducktails combed them in such a way that they met in the back and were perfectly centered and parted in the back of their heads. I, for the life of me, could never figure out how to achieve this affectation. Did they use a mirror, or enlist the aid of a sibling or parent in this effort? My brother, Terry, was a big proponent of this hairstyle without the part in the back. Apparently, he couldn't figure it out either. Since both of us suffered from the same deficiency, I reached the logical conclusion that it was due to a genetic shortcoming. Terry had so much grease on his head that, in a pinch, he could have lubricated his '57 Chevy.

There was only one place to get one's haircut if you wanted to have any neighborhood authenticity, Sal's Barber Shop on St. John Avenue just east of Van Brunt. It was a generic fifties store front on the south side of the elm lined street. Anyplace else was for sissies and old men, and you'd be laughed off the basketball court with any haircut that didn't come from Sal's. Somehow, the other kids could tell. As you walked past the red, white and blue spinning barber pole, you were assaulted with the flowery odors of hair tonics and lotions fused with the cheap panatellas and Lucky Strikes. Usually everyone in the place over the age of 12, including the barbers, were smoking. There were four chairs at Sal's. Sal had the first chair and was booked up for years in advance. There was usually an immaculate big finned Cadillac parked out front

and some fat guy with a stogey in his face, his shirt unbuttoned at the top to display his impressive crop of chest hair on which a crucifix suspended on a delicate chain rested. He sported a flashy pinky ring, socks that you could see through covered by the latest style of Florshiem shoes, (We *peons* bought our shoes at Flagg Brothers or Thom McCann.) He got the whole treatment, his face hidden by the pre-shave hot towel. He would pay Sal from a massive wad of large denomination bills secured by a large pink rubber band that he pulled out of the pocket of his shiny shark-skin slacks. Sometimes, guys would come in and hand Sal money without benefit of having received any service whatsoever.

Second chair was Sal's Dad, Dominic, who enjoyed a similar clientele. None of us kids ever got our hair cut by Sal or Dominic. Third chair was Gene, a terrific barber, who was not Italian. He was relegated to the walk-in trade. Gene cut my hair until the late '60s when I followed the trend among musicians and let it grow long.

There was an elderly black man, bald, with a salt and pepper horseshoe fringe who addressed everyone as "Boss". He had a shoeshine chair and every color shoe polish and every kind of brush ever made. He was usually squatting, putting a sheen on the Florsheims of the guy in Sal's chair. I once put up the dough to have him shine my tasseled loafers just before a dance. My shoes never looked better.

The magazines were the latest Field and Stream, Sports Illustrated, or Motor Trend. There were also countless dog-eared comic books. When we were younger, we could trade our comic books to Sal, two for one in his favor. It was a way to stretch a dollar's worth of comics from 10 to 15. By 13 though, I wouldn't have been caught dead with a comic. I was heavily into Jules Verne and H. G. Wells. The radio blared rock 'n roll from WHB, the only sanctioned station of Northeast youth. It was a steady flow of Bill Haley and the Comets, Rockin'

Around the Clock, or pretty boy Pat Boone's honey dripping tenor juxtaposed to a back-beat singing
"Little Richard" tunes like "Tutti Fruitti". We got Boone instead of Richard because WHB rarely ever played black artists or what was referred to in the trade as "race music". (This would change with Chuck Berry.) Every girl in my freshman "Common Learnings" class had a picture of Pat Boone taped to one of their books. The boy wasn't that much of a singer, but he was good looking, much more so than Little Richard. But his time was running out. Elvis and Ricky Nelson loomed!

My brother and friends, Chuck and Jim, all looked good in flat-tops, so I decided to give it a try. I got one flat-top in my life, and when Gene, my barber, held the mirror up for my approval, I was horrified. Being painfully thin with a big nose and ears that suck out, I looked like "Mr. Potato Head" on a popsicle stick. I had realized fifteen minutes too late that I did not have a flat-top face. Fortunately this ill-advised experiment was in the summer and I had plenty of time for it to grow out before school, or I would have had to implement a hat to cover my blunder. I was saved from neighborhood ridicule by the fact that my family was leaving for Minnesota for a fishing vacation the next day. My Dad had booked us into a mosquito and tick preserve called Webb Lake. He fished while Mom, Terry and I sat around bored while being eaten alive.

I never made that fashion mistake again. From then on it was Elvis style pompadours *sans* sideburns. Taking umbrage at my hair length, my Dad would yell, “What did you buy with the money I gave you for a haircut?” I would always reply, “I bought a haircut”, which just made him more angry. I had considered sideburns, but that would have gotten me excommunicated. (Even Elvis, at the urging of the RCA Records marketing department, parted ways with his truck-driver sideburns.)

There was always a wait at Sal’s. Business was good. Sports was always the

topic, baseball and boxing. While Mickey Mantle was good, he was not the equivalent of Joe DiMaggio, “The Yankee Clipper”. The other paragon was Rocky Marciano, the only heavyweight to retire undefeated at 49-0. In Sal’s eyes he was the greatest fighter of all time. These two were sacrosanct and enshrined in pictures on Sal’s wall. To not show them the proper respect would have gotten you banned from Sal’s. One guy interjected his opinion that Joe Lewis was the greatest fighter. A furious Sal snapped right back, “Bullshit - Rocky knocked that fungee through the ropes back in ‘51.” The offending guy waited so long for a haircut that he finally got up and left. (Sal failed to make allowance for the fact that Joe was 37, hadn't fought in two years and was coming out of retirement because of huge indebtedness to the always gracious Internal Revenue Service. Opportunities for African-Americans to make large sums of money were extremely limited in those days. I guess the IRS would rather have had Joe killed in the ring than give him a break.)

During my sophomore year, the high school hero jocks all started wearing their hair extremely short, maybe an eighth of an inch from a shave job. Not wanting to commit the same blunder twice, I was sticking with my pompadour. However, Terry, always the iconoclast, and because of his status on the track team, decide to appropriate this look for himself and enlisted Gene's help in this matter. Gene hit the mark, but then he was the one who had cut all those kid's hair. When Terry came home, Mom erupted. She was a human Vesuvius screaming, "Have you lost your mind?" She instructed him to go right back to the barber shop. Always the mediator, I pointed out that while Gene was a terrific barber, not even he had the power to miraculously restore the hair to a kid's head. I also stated the obvious, that this was all very temporary and that Terry's head would be back to normal in a couple of weeks. This did not placate Mom. Terry did what he always did when caught red handed, he blamed someone else. "I think maybe Gene was drunk." Being fully cognizant of the situation, I immediately came to Gene's defense. Gene had cut my hair right after Terry's and had done a fine job and I had noticed no liquor fumes or diminished capacity whatsoever. Mom called up Gene and gave him hell anyway. That evening, Dad, weighed in on the matter. "Can't either one of you just get a normal god damned haircut? Ronnie looks like they didn't take anything off, and Terry looks like he's been scalped." The next time I got my haircut Gene told me he had just followed Terry's instructions and had wondered what had transpired. I told him that I had no doubt of his veracity in this matter.

As I matured, I began to realize that the only constant in life is change. And the neighborhood was changing. The big houses up on Gladstone Boulevard and Sunset Drive, where it was rumored that mobsters lived, turned over, and the people of dubious reputations moved to a compound in North Kansas City. Sal sold the shop to Gene and he and Dominic followed their clientele to Northtown. And that was the end of an era. The shop was never the same after that. No local characters, no bets, no Cadillacs outside and no heated sports arguments. Gene was a great barber, but the only thing that happened after Sal's exodus was haircuts.

Chapter 11 "The Great Northeast Ice Cream Eating Contest of 1959"

My family loved desserts - cookies, pies, cobblers, cakes, short cake, pudding - you name it. If it had sugar in it and whipped cream on top, we had it, one with every meal except breakfast. I'd even been known, when Mom wasn't looking, to top off my Wheaties with a purloined sliver of cherry pie. But our all-time favorite, and it wasn't close, was ice cream. The best was when, on a hot summer day, Dad would crank the handle on the old arm powered ice cream making machine with a canister of ice cream in the middle, surrounded by ice and toped off with rock salt. As the mixture thickened and the crank became harder to turn, Dad would have Terry or me sit on top to hold the machine in place while he cranked, which resulted in a very cold bohuncus. That, my friends, was ice cream, and worth all the trouble it took to make it. We made several varieties - we added strawberries to the mix, or Hershey's chocolate syrup, or Nestle's chocolate chips. You were tying up 30 minutes of cranking time plus putting the raw materials together. It was for special occasions, definitely not an every day thing. Terry, at a very young age, showed an extraordinary ability to devour huge quantities of ice cream. Of the available commercial ice creams, the apogee was Velvet Freeze cherry-vanilla. (The designer ice cream boutiques, Ben and Jerry's or Haagen Daz, or the 28 flavors of Baskin and Robbins didn't exist in those days.)

Sometimes, in the summer, we'd have a post desert, desert. While we watched the Gillette Cavalcade of Sports, we would run back on a commercial and make sundaes with Velvet Freeze Golden Vanilla ice-cream and Smucker's toppings. (As a lad, I was fascinated with the idea that somewhere, there was a woman called "Mother Smucker".) Home air conditioning didn't exist in our world. The green Emerson window fan and all the windows up was the best we were going to get. On really hot summer nights, we'd schlep on down to the air conditioned Velvet Freeze, take our place at the end of queue, which was usually out past the door and the sidewalk, wait impatiently to, first, get inside to cool off, and then to order. We practically always got hot fudge sundaes with whipped cream and a cherry on top.

Mom's first refrigerator was a General Electric that was a huge improvement over the old oak ice box we had used. The GE usually contained ice cream if Mom could keep Terry out of it.

Dad, who was always scouting out new places to eat, discovered the Country Club Dairy at 57th and Troost. Country Club was a local brand of milk and other dairy products including a very good ice cream. They featured excellent banana splits and their signature concoction,

"The Flying Saucer". It was a huge sundae featuring incredible hot fudge, in a pot metal dish with a paper cone insert and topped with whipped cream and a cherry. It was the holy grail. A bad week could be immediately transformed into a good one with a trip to the Country Club Dairy. The Flying Saucer had great powers!

We kids of the fifties were underprivileged in that we had only three channels of television with unreliable rabbit ear antennae, no cable, cell phones, Ipods, computers, internet and no video games. To cool off, my pal, Chuck Tye, would go so far as to set up a washtub full of ice water, then position an electric fan so that it blew across the tub and cool, moist air onto him as he sat in a reclining chair in front of the TV. We had to actually think of something to do. One particularly hot summer night, Terry and I were up at Jim Sander's house. We all had jobs by then. I delivered hot bread to the steam table line at the Forum Cafeteria, Terry was a stock-boy at Sears and Jim delivered the Northeast News, so we had some money. Jim's younger brother, Jack, was there and another friend, Mike O'Brien. We decided to go to Mecca, the Country Club Dairy. We all got into my powder blue and white '54 Chevy Bel Air. (I had started working at Agron's Market at 13, and had saved money for years for this prize.) We drove the fifteen minute trip and waited for a spot at the counter. They only had bar type seats, no tables. After what seemed like an era, five seats finally became available and we pounced.

The Country Club Dairy displayed their chilly treats in a slick color menu with a picture of a virtual cornucopia of multi-colored dips of ice cream. I made the off-handed comment that no one could possibly eat that much ice cream. That met with immediate derision from Jim and Terry, both very competitive individuals, who were proud of their consumptive prowess. A careful count of the dips in the picture revealed that there were 46 dips of ice cream. Confident that I couldn't lose, I proclaimed boldly that if anyone could eat 46 dips, that I would pay for it. I got an immediate response from four takers. Being 5'11 ½" and weighing 128 pounds, I knew, absolutely, that this Herculean feat was well beyond my capability. We polished off our Flying Saucers and set the date for the event, the following Thursday afternoon.

We decided on the Velvet Freeze at St. John and Belmont for the eat-off, because it was less crowded than the alternatives. On the way, we established the rules. Failure to eat for two minutes was grounds for disqualification, as was regurgitation. The ice cream would be ordered in five dip increments to simplify scorekeeping. Each order would be in a clean dish so all we had to do was count each participant's empty dishes to simplify the tally. There were four contestants, Terry, Jim, Jack and Mike. I was the referee, judge, timekeeper and scorekeeper. At five cents a dip, if all four contestants reached their goal, I would be out $9.20, about half of my week's salary at the Forum. Terry, always the gambler, and maybe having some second thoughts about his *braggadocio*, tried to leverage his wager with some side bets as to which of the four ice creamers would prevail.

There was a rainbow of colors in three of the dishes, but Terry, fearing that mixing the flavors might cause some gastrointestinal distress, adhered to a strict vanilla only diet. The quartet breezed easily through the first dish without mishap and moved on to the second. Jack, who was younger, and much smaller, hit the wall at seven dips. The third dishes were ordered and the competition intensified. Terry and Jim were still going strong, but Mike was beginning to look a little queasy. The fourth dishes were served and Mike stopped eating for a minute and a half, but got a second wind and ate two more dips, at which point, looking like a sailor in the aftermath of a two day bender, threw in his spoon. He had shoved down a respectable 17 dips. Undaunted, Jim and Terry roared on, spoons blazing, twenty-five, thirty, then thirty-five dips. I was beginning to doubt the sapience of my rash statement. Then Jim ate the 36th dip, got up and in a full sprint, ran outside and barfed all over the sidewalk. Terry looked up at Jim, heaving, shook his head and kept right on eating.

"It was the sherbet," Terry proclaimed with absolute certainty. "He shouldn't have mixed them, he should have stuck with straight ice cream."

I was sorry for my friend Jim's discomfort, but was relieved that my potential liability had been reduced by half. It was smooth sailing for Terry, right up to dip number forty. By then we had drawn quite a crowd of both employees and fellow ice cream lovers who all looked on in amazement. Terry was not a large person at that time, being 5'10" and weighing in at 145. Terry took a short break, then picked up dish number nine. He ripped trough dip 41, but at dip 42 his enthusiasm began to wane. Fading, he stared at the dip, nibbled at it a bit, then sheepishly declared, "That's it. I don't want to get sick." I was very relieved. It was a much closer contest then I had anticipated, but I had dodged the bullet. I never dreamed anyone would get past 25. Everyone paid the clerk who declared "You boys were real nice. You can have your ice cream eating contests here any time." Then a man walked over to Terry and said, "Son, that's the damnedest thing I've ever seen." He handed Terry a half gallon of vanilla and said, "The next one's on me.

Terry never got sick and later that night ate a full dinner. I not only didn't have to pay, I had really enjoyed my double dip cone of raspberry revel and had a great afternoon's entertainment for free.

In a recent discussion of this event, Terry laughed and said, "I couldn't even feel my tongue."

I have told this story many times through the years, but no one can remember anyone even approaching 42 dips, or having the desire to do so.

Chapter 12 "Twinkle Toes Roberts: My Incredibly Short Dancing Career"

E. Floyd Connerley was like our social director. He was resourceful, optimistic, involved, curious and always had a big Irish grin on his face. He could always think of something to do and was always there for a ride to a game or a trip to the Dairy Way. He was really enjoying his senior year. As a Junior, I was not that happy. I was a dreamer with a head full of musical ideas and visions of Broadway and Hollywood (both dreams would come true.) I knew that this was not my place and time. I was always confident that good things waited in the wings, but they weren't there now, and I was just putting in my time, living vicariously, anticipating something, somewhere down the line. In the vernacular of my trade, I was paying my dues. My nose was always buried in a book, or I'd be watching some old Noir black and white movie with Humphrey Bogart or Robert Mitchum on television. I didn't yet have my own car which was a prerequisite for any kind of dating life. I was taking speech courses and Latin, (which would be of no use in my later life) courses that the counselor had recommended for someone headed toward pre-law in college.

Floyd was saving me from myself. He could always talk me into doing something that turned out to be fun, like the Inter Society Dance.

He said I should go. I told him I didn't have a car or a girlfriend, so what was the point? He went so far as to fix me up with a really cute girl, Jane, from Raytown, and I had a really good time. Floyd even talked Dad into loaning us a '58 Ford convertible for the evening. I wore my white sport coat that I had bought at Montgomery Wards for $12 in anticipation of just such an occasion.

Floyd, at that time was an aspiring actor and he managed to get a speaking part in a really good play, "Inherit the Wind", at Kansas City University, a major coup for a high school student. Then he talked me into doing several non-speaking walk-on parts, which turned out to be quite amusing. I got to wear a boater and a white with navy blue pin-striped suit, carry a sign that said "We're not apes" (the play was about the famous Scopes' trial about teaching the theory of evolution) and sing "When the rolllll…is called up yonderrr" with a chorus. They gooped up my hair and parted it in the middle, '30's style.

Floyd and I both had Miss Seur for Public Speaking, who was a pert, energetic young lady, with her black, pixie hair cut, that we both admired. Miss Seur had been assigned to coordinate the "Viking Varieties", the annual talent show. I was already signed up, singing and playing guitar on Elvis's "As Long As I have You" (I'm sure this would have been quite an affront to the great Elvis) and playing bass for a girl's vocal trio. Floyd had a colossal crush on a really great looking Senior named Doralee. She was an elegant beauty, very sophisticated, with a natural honey tan complexion, soft, light-brown curls, and eyes that laughed. Her wardrobe suggested family affluence. Floyd never had even a Hail Mary of a chance, but he gave it his all anyway. Miss Seur's boyfriend was a dance instructor who volunteered to choreograph a dance routine for the show. Miss Seur had no trouble getting female volunteers, but the only male was E. Floyd. Doralee was one of the female volunteers and that was the only incentive E. Floyd needed. He saw that as his big chance (he never had any). He appointed himself as Doralee's partner and began recruiting his friends to fill the other three slots. The dance routine was pretty hokey, something called the "Tower Trot". Floyd started working on me relentlessly. He reminded me of how much fun the play had been. I replied that seeing myself as an actor, like maybe Humphrey Bogart/Phillip Marlow, driving up to the Sternwood Mansion in a 36 Plymouth Business Coupe with a trap door in the dashboard that held a secret .38 caliber Smith & Wesson, was a concept I could get behind. However, Fred Astaire was another matter and off the radar. Floyd reminded me of my musical talent. I replied that my talent's source was my brain and that the circuit extended to my hands, but it came to a screeching halt, abruptly at my waist. Floyd wouldn't let go. We all liked going bowling, and he and Miss Seur worked it out so that the rehearsals would be at the King Louie Bowling Lanes and we'd get free bowling afterwards. I replied that the possibility of me making a fool of myself in front of the student body, dancing, was not worth a few lines of free bowling. He offered me five bucks. I still held my ground. I reminded him that I already had two scheduled performances , doing something that I was actually kind of good at and that was enough. He backed off for a little while, but then in a few days, he got me cornered and hit me with his haymaker. He indicated that he had two of the guys he needed lined up and I was costing him his chance to dance with the dazzling Doralee. Then he said the magic words, that they needed a partner for Toni. I was stunned and asked in disbelief, "Who did you say?" "Toni," Floyd replied as a huge grin spread across his curly haired Irish mug. He knew he had me. Toni was an incredibly cute, perky Italian girl with a radiant personality, a Senior, perhaps the most popular girl in the school. She also was kind to everyone, had a really sweet disposition and always seemed to be bursting with happiness, and, oh yes, she could really dance. She was a black haired angel. While I always had an abundance of confidence, it was in my talent and intelligence. It definitely did not extend to my appearance. I was 5' 11 ¾" and, at that time, weighed 128. I was a bean pole with a nose that far exceeded standard issue. I was amazed that they couldn't find one of the pretty-boys to dance with Toni. I have never been one to miss an opportunity when it occurs, or question good fortune in any manner, so I said yes. Inspired by Toni, I threw myself into rehearsals and actually begin to get the routine. I couldn't dance like Ray, one of the other fellows, but I was getting by, and Tony was very magnanimous about any shortcoming I might have.

After rehearsals began, one day in Orchestra class, they asked for volunteers to go on the local version of a "Bandstand" show. Each show featured teenagers from a different high school with local M C, John Bilyou, dancing to hit records, and they had gotten around to Northeast. I didn't give it much thought, but then, Gail, a bass clarinet player and friend, grabbed my arm and said we should go. When I reacted with a certain lack of enthusiasm, she urged, "Oh come on. Be a sport. We'll get out of class early and get to be on TV. Won't that be fun?" Gail's fervor was contagious, as was the prospect of an excused absence in a boring class or two. I had never been on television before and I decided that since I already had an embryonic show business career going, the experience would be a good thing. Gail and I volunteered as a couple. Fate, it seemed, had made a unilateral decision that I should become a dancer. I figured I would maneuver to the back of the pack, inconspicuously, to where my deficiency in dancing chops wouldn't be noticeable. The next day a school bus came for us and the "Bandstand" crew piled in. I found a place and sat with my partner, Gail. Sitting across the aisle was my friend Densel, a Benton brother. He grabbed my arm and said, "Hey Ron. Ask Gail if she has any makeup I could use?"

"What? What do you need with makeup?"

"When I volunteered yesterday, my complexion was clear. I got up this morning and I saw this huge zit right in the middle of my forehead." I scoped out his forehead, and he was right. It was a monster of epic proportions, approaching a world record, no doubt. Gail did have a compact with some face powder that she applied to Densel's mother of all pimples. It did little good.

"I think, I'll just wait outside. I don't want to be on TV with this zit."

Densel was a handsome fellow, and like most good looking people, just a little vain about his appearance. I thought it was pretty funny so I told him that I had done some acting and knew something of photography, and that I was certain that it wouldn't even show up on black and white TV. (This was pure malarkey!) Gail picked up on my cue and told him that if he missed this chance that he'd regret it when he got older. Densel finally decided to go ahead and go on in.

We filed off the bus and went into the channel 9 studio at 10th and Central. They told us the tunes they'd be playing and said we should just relax and have fun, and that we shouldn't try to look toward the camera, or anything, that we should just be ourselves. The cameraman knew what to do. The show started and I had to admit that being on TV was exciting. Much to my alarm, I soon discovered that Gail was a terrific dancer, which made me look even worse. In desperation, I worked my way toward the rear, then I saw a monitor. There right in the middle, with a full head shot, was Densel, really tearing it up, twirling his partner to Chuck Berry's "Maybelene". The zit on his forehead, not only showed, it looked like Mt. Vesuvius. TV had a magnifying effect and it had an existence of its own that took over the screen! I started laughing, and figured that if I screwed up, at least it wouldn't be with this humongous pustule right in the middle of my head like some kind of pink third eye. No one would be looking at me anyway, they'd all be gazing on in utter amazement at that monumental zit. The rest of the show went fine, then they thanked us, gave us all a Snickers, headed us back on the bus and took us back to Northeast.

Viking Varieties loomed and in preparation for the big night, I went to Thom McCann's and bought myself a pair of spiffy black tasseled loafers. You can't be a hoofer in worn down wing tips! I polished them to a high sheen! I wore my white sport coat. The show night came and I was apprehensive in Floyd's Mercury as we drove to the school. We parked and took our place backstage. As the spotlights came on and the eight of us pranced out, I wondered why I had gotten myself into this. I was as nervous as a mallard on the first day of hunting season. My apprehensions about the dance routine were misplaced. The performance went fine and we got a nice round of applause. The night's mishap occurred as I came out to sing "As Long As I Have You", from "King Creole" which was, at that time, my favorite movie. My guitar strap

slipped and I almost dropped my precious Harmony electric arch-top guitar that I had worked so hard to pay for. My friend Doug said he could read my lips and I had said "Son-of-a-bitch", fortunately off mike, in front of the whole audience. I recovered my composure and did the tune. Floyd had been right again. It had been a grand night. Then the 1959 annual came out, and there I was on the 3rd page, chronicled in perpetuity, doing something I was really bad at, dancing my way into their hearts with darling Toni. That was the end of my two performance dancing career. I never liked to dance, I was always the guy in the band. But Gail and Toni made it fun. They both graduated a year before me and I never saw either of them again, nor did E. Floyd ever see Doralee.

In 1970, my dream had become my reality. I had been playing bass and doing back-up vocals and arranging for a great singer, Kay Dennis, and we had an album out and a national tour booked. We were playing the Penthouse at the downtown Hilton, the highest paid act at the best room in town. As we finished the set and I was putting up my bass I heard, "Ronnie" (I had been trying to distance myself from the moniker since Jr. High), and turned to see the lovely Doralee, looking *tres chic* in a tailored white dress and an Edith Head type big hat. She had married a Floridian. We had a very pleasant visit reminiscing back to 1959. That was the last time I saw her.

Chapter 13 "Grand Theft Auto"

My high school buddy, Tommy, was an incredible goofball. He was always doing something that, while not criminal in nature, was sometimes borderline, and generally hilarious. At Northeast High, firecrackers were a beloved commodity, and we always had plenty of ordinance thanks to a classmate, George, another of the half Italians, who was a firework's wholesaler. George was always rolling in dough. He and his Dad would spend their summers in states where fireworks were illegal, set up a makeshift roadside stand, make a few hundred selling fireworks at super-inflated prices, then scram before the local fuzz got wind of the operation. We could always get anything we wanted from George and the top of the food chain was the ubiquitous M-80. Just short of a hand grenade, it made the popular cherry bomb look like a cap pistol. One of Tommy's favorite tricks was to flush a lit M-80 down a toilet (yes, gunpowder burns underwater). Water does not compress so the subsequent explosion invariably blew the crapper right off the wall. One could hear the report all over the building and the water flowing from under the men's room door usually meant that Tommy had struck again. Tommy was not capricious in this activity - he always had some provocation, usually an 8th hour he felt he didn't deserve, or a social slight of some sort.

Another of Tommy's favorite stunts was to get someone with a fast car to drive him around Cliff Drive, to lover's lane, which was usually referred to as "pecker point". He would bide his time till he saw a car in which no heads visible, and with an amazing control that would have made Don Drysdale proud, he would one hop an M-80 with a lit cigarette attached to the fuse, under it. The cigarette would take several minutes to burn down to the fuse, allowing Tommy to be far away when the ensuing explosion convinced the car's occupants that gang warfare had broken out. It usually brought any foreplay to a screeching-assed halt. Tommy felt that as long as he wasn't getting any action, well, no one else should either.

Tommy had two younger siblings, a brother and a sister, who were both as adorable as

six week old kittens. To make matters worse, they were always on the honor roll. No one ever viewed Tommy as anywhere near adorable. Tommy lived in one of the big stone houses on Benton that even had a bar in the basement. It was his practice to host a Saturday night poker game there, every week, for the guys who were already well on their way to becoming degenerate gamblers, or the losers, like him, who couldn't get a date. (I frequented these because I worked till 8:30 at the Forum

Cafeteria and it was too late to do anything else.) Terry was usually the big winner.

Tommy was never a threat to make the honor roll. He was smart enough, but felt so alienated and disenfranchised, that he would have needed radar to even find it. He was devoid of any academic interest or curiosity. He also could not thrive in a highly structured, rigid environment. That didn't sit well with his over-achiever Mom, who viewed Tommy's disinterest as a serious character deficiency. As a result, she showered praise and money on the two younger siblings, but was on Tommy's case pretty much 24/7. Tommy felt that his Mother didn't treat him properly, and those of us who spent any time at his house tended to agree with him.

Tommy got into a huge confrontation with her. Most of his friends had cars, albeit generally some old derelict Ford that had seen better days a decade ago. Tommy's Mom's position was that the right to a car had to be earned and the only path ran right through the honor roll. Tommy strongly disagreed, and he couldn't just buy his own like I had because she wouldn't let him work till his grades met her standards. (Let's face it, Tommy's grades weren't even up to my standards, which was to keep everything in the general area of Cs with as little effort as possible, and I always had had a stellar memory so this didn't require any great expenditure of energy. I had long ago located that fine line and had it down cold. I was just a .bit alienated myself. At 16, I had declared my independence, was bored with high school and sick of adults telling me what to do and the regimentation.

This battle of wills between Tommy and his Mom was ongoing and of ever increasing intensity. Tommy's Mom was a big shot in the P.T.A. and with a doctor husband, was the fashion plate of the neighborhood, and drove a Cadillac which she would barely let Tommy ride in, let alone drive. She all but ran the massive Independence Boulevard Christian Church. (Nothing but a strait jacket and a pair of well-muscled attendants could have gotten Tommy anywhere near that building.) Tommy was a constant source of embarrassment and consternation for her. What wacky stunt would he pull next? She would never give him any spending money and this coupled with her refusal to let him work, had him completely boxed in. To meet his needs, Tommy became a master shoplifter. He was so light fingered that he never got caught. (He wouldn't have cared if he had.) One night he was sent to the Katz Drugstore at 39th and Main to pick up something for his Mom. He became furious when he couldn't get a clerk to wait on him. (Service at Katz was always lackadaisical at best.) Then inspiration struck. He filched the entire record department, making trip after trip with the albums under his overcoat. He then gave them all away at that night's poker game. I still have my copy of Martin Denny's "Enchanted Island" that he gave me. I'm assuming that the statute of limitations on "receiving stolen property" has long expired.

The car stand-off got more hostile and Tommy was resourceful. He decided that if he wasn't going to get a car then his Mom must pay, and the thing that she valued most was her social standing and dignity.

One of the best cars in the neighborhood was Donnie Nelson's '56 Ford convertible.

It had three deuces, dual exhaust with glass-packs, chrome full length Lake's Pipes, sat maybe an inch and a half off the ground and had a full set of '56 Oldsmobile Fiesta spinner hub caps. Its flashy metallic emerald paint job was so bright, and was polished to such a high luster, that

viewing it without your Ray-Bans could result in retinal trauma. Everyone at Northeast High knew that car. Donnie, with his oiled up ducktails, low hanging Levis, black motorcycle boots and a white tee shirt with a pack of Chesterfields rolled up in the left sleeve, and one dangling from his lip, was constantly cruising through every drive-in, with the top down and a full load of surly teenagers. Tommy was turning magenta with envy. Then inspiration struck. He would take matters into his own hands. He staked out Donnie's house, timing his comings and goings. He determined that Donnie usually rolled in about midnight, after the drive-ins closed. After he had completed his research, he lay in wait one night , and after Donnie parked the Ford and went inside, Tommy gave him some time to get into a deep slumber. Then he sprang. He fashioned a wire coat hangar and worked it between the glass and the rubber in the vent window and snagged the door handle. He then hot-wired the car, put it in neutral and coasted down the hill. The pipes were so loud that firing up the hopped-up V-8 would have alerted Donnie. When he was a safe distance away he jump started the big 312 cubic inch mill, then spent the night cruising and drag racing other crepuscular youths at stop lights. Tommy knew that come daylight, the car would be missed, reported to the police and an all points bulletin would be issued. Then he'd be a wanted man. But that was part of the master plan. He parked it down by Green Lake on Cliff Drive, under Black Bridge and grabbed a little shut-eye in the back seat. When he woke up he found a pay phone and called the police. He told them he had the car and that he would surrender himself at precisely 12:30 in front of Independence Boulevard Christian Church. This was exactly the time that church let out and his Mom would be coming out the front door, preening, for all of her important friends. Then he hid out and waited for the glorious moment. At 12:30 PM he pulled up in front of the massive gothic façade, parked the green convertible in the middle of Independence Avenue and shut down the motor. In an instant cops came from every direction, a paddy wagon showed up, and before Tommy could say Jack Robinson, they muscled him out of the car, and had him spread-eagled against the paddy wagon, patting him down. Before they got the hand-cuffs on him, he managed to get one hand free, waved, and yelled "Hi, Mom" just as she walked out of church, surrounded by her usual entourage. As they loaded him in the paddy wagon, he had a satisfied smile on his face, having tasted the sweet nectar of vengeance.

Not much happened as a result of the theft. In a poor neighborhood like mine, nobody much liked the cops. Donnie, who was what the establishment would have called a juvenile delinquent (He paid for customizing his Ford via the midnight auto supply and his basement looked like a Western Auto store,) was of this persuasion. He had his car back without any damage which was the only thing he wanted. Showing both a sense of humor, and being what the Northeast toughs called, "a stand-up guy", he refused to press charges, so the heat had to kick Tommy loose. After a day or so, Tommy was back on the street, hosting his Saturday night poker game, a man of the world, enlightening his young admirers about what is was like to be in the slammer, and basking in his new-found fame. He was the talk of the town, but he still didn't have a car. That pretty much terminated his relationship with his Mom, which was okay by Tommy. He had long been prepared to write it off.

I ran into him about ten years after this episode. I owned a small record store and Tommy came in to buy some sides. Always blessed with the gift of gab, he was working as a traveling salesman for a manufacturer. When I asked about his family, he just made a face.

Chapter 14 "At Last It Can Be Told"

The big Northeast mystery of the fifties, outside of several mafia executions and constant petty theft via the midnight auto supply, was who blew up the Cliff Drive Spring. Cliff Drive was a beautiful, narrow, winding two lane road around the wooded bluff facing the Missouri River. It snaked eastward from The Paseo for maybe three miles, past Green Lake which was covered with a scum, algae most likely, under an emerald umbrella of overhanging tree foliage on both sides. Near the end was a spring which consisted of an alcove that had been carved out of the rock strata, a concrete base on which rested a cement basin under a metal, constantly flowing spigot that would fill the basin with water, which overflowed into a drain. People used to come up there with gallon jugs to get a supply of free spring water. Two sports became a part of Northeast folklore. Number one was careening around Cliff Drive at insane speeds trying to get the smallest elapsed time. (Okay, we were idiots.) George had the record with his bronze '57 Chevy with the covered in chrome Corvette engine. (We were all full of testosterone fired certainty, that given a seat in A. J. Foyt's car, and an hour to practice, any one of us could have won the Indianapolis 500. We personified reckless youth.) Number two was trying to, on the fly, from an open car window, land an M-80 in the spring basin, the object of which was to get as big a splash as possible. This was usually an exercise in futility, but on occasion, some deadeye got lucky.

I think, at some point in life, every young man has a fascination with explosives; that's why there are fireworks and why, in movies, things are constantly being exploded. As a tyke, I loved watching trains blow up in Randolph Scott westerns, and everything else go off in John Wayne war movies at "Double Feature with 8 Cartoons" Saturday matinees at the Vista, Benton or Gladstone theaters.

We didn't have to wait for the 4th of July to stock up on ordinance. We had George. He could get us anything we wanted at any time, pin-wheels, bottle rockets, cherry bombs... The weapon of choice was the always popular M-80, just short of a blasting cap. All my friends had them. We would throw them under cars at lover's lane as we sped around Cliff Drive for our nightly shot at the Cliff Drive Spring. While the M-80 was the biggest legal firecracker, and extremely loud, like standing next to a 12 gauge shotgun, it really wasn't big enough to cause any real damage to anything. Phil Harris, who was a mean-spirited peripheral player in my group of friends, had access to the second fastest car, his step-dad's powder blue '57 Oldsmobile hardtop with the high performance J-2 engine with 3 two barrel carburetors. He decided to up the ante. One M-80 would produce a big splash. So he came up with the idea of taping two together and winding the fuses around each other and then gluing them with rubber cement to insure a simultaneous explosion. This not only doubled the bang, but greatly enhanced the splash. This satisfied him for a while, but Phil wasn't the highest watt bulb on the shelf. He decided he'd try something even more spectacular. He got an empty glass prescription bottle and proceeded to make his own hand grenade. He had done some research and discovered that loose gunpowder doesn't explode, it just fizzles. It has to be compressed in a confined space, so he opened five M-80s to get enough powder to fill the bottle, drilled a hole in a rubber stopper for the fuse and then sealed the whole gizmo with rubber cement. One of our friends, Bob, who unlike Phil, was quite bright and a good chemistry student, told Phil he was a moron and would probably blow his balls off. This in no way discouraged Phil. He drove out to a place by Parkville where we used to go shooting with George's extensive gun collection and tested a few to fine tune his design. Then he was ready for the next step.

At this point in my life, the hormones had kicked in big-time and I was a lot more interested in teenage girls than blowing things up with firecrackers. I viewed this as maturity, something Phil was singularly lacking. I had gotten out of the prankster's loop in favor of pursuing, unsuccessfully, a cute freckle-faced redhead named Evelyn, who was a year older than me. Spring at Northeast High was a special time because of the annual literary contest called "Lit Night". To participate in this event, you had to be a member of one of the Literary societies. Fraternities and Sororities had long ago been outlawed by the Kansas City School District. To get around this, the idea of Literary Societies had been born. They were nothing but a front for the aforementioned. I had never had much interest in these, but in 1958, my friend, Floyd, convinced me of the social benefits: lots of parties with really cute girls, rides to football games, etc. He told me that no chick could resist a society man, so I became a Benton. (Plenty of them resisted me). There were six of these clubs at Northeast, two for boys, the Bentons and the Debaters, and four for girls, the Alphas, Clios, Deltas and Thetas. The big Literary contest involved much preparation. Essays, poems and short stories had to be written and declamations and orations had to be selected and rehearsed. That was the serious side of it, which was a minor factor indeed. It was an excuse to indulge in a month's worth of parties and pranks. As a prelude to the literary contest, each society was given a specific time to sing songs with lyrics they had written in self praise . It preparation for this, song practices and writing sessions were held. These were kept secret to keep other societies from implementing practical jokes, a Northeast tradition. After one of our song practices, George said he had clandestine information on where and when the Delta song practice was being held, at out friend Sue's house, This was big because the Deltas were the sister society to the Debaters, our arch-rivals. George said he had worked all day preparing a special device for just such an occasion. He had made a string of a gross (144) of M-80's connected to a common fuse so that they would detonate in rapid succession. He was looking for a couple of volunteers to execute this maneuver. Herbie and I stepped up. We used George's '57 Chevy with the Corvette mill. No one could catch that car. George drove over to Sue's house which sat in the middle of a lot and was surrounded by a wrought iron fence. We climbed over the fence, then crawled, commando style, and strung the device completely around the house. George had come prepared and he connected a long fuse so the gizmo could be ignited from beyond the fence. He lit it and we sped off. It sounded like the allied landing at Normandy beach, ka-boom, boom, boom...

Shortly after that, Cecil and Ed came up with the mother of all Lit Night jokes. Ed had this garden sprayer that looked like a bicycle pump, except it had two hoses. You place one hose in a tub of water and then pumped the handle. Out of the other hose came a big jet of water that sprayed about 40 feet. Cecil had a '51 Studebaker four-door sedan that had an immense space between the front and rear seats. He pointed out at a Benton's meeting that a metal wash tub would fit in there. Two guys could ride in the back seat, one pumping, the other aiming the hose and fire a stream of water big enough to soak anyone, many times over, firing at will. The next logical question was who should we pull this on? Someone said that they knew where and when a Theta song practice was being held. Floyd pitched in that Roberts (me) could bring his guitar and we could serenade the Thetas while hiding water balloons under our Benton jackets. Ed and Cecil and a driver could have the Studebaker already in place. When they came out to see who was singing, we could open fire. This met with enthusiastic and unanimous approval.

The big night came. We prepared a huge stash of water balloons that were distributed. About 25 of us piled into several cars and we parked about a block from the house so as not to arouse suspicion. We strolled over and lined up and I plucked my guitar strings…

"Love me tender, love me true,
Never let me go…"

Out came the Thetas, maybe 20 of them, unable to resist our manly harmony. Just as we hit the second chorus, Ed and Cecil opened up from the Studie. They had found a perfect spot right in front of the house. The water balloons didn't do that much damage, but, boy, the water

sprayer did. There were a bunch of very soaked Thetas. We all cleared out. Later a jock with an IQ slightly below that of the average sand flea, caught up with one of our guys and nearly put his

eye out with a well aimed knuckle sandwich. Now the thing about practical jokes is that revenge should be proportionate to the offense, and in kind. To seriously injure someone and subsequently be convicted of felony assault is the height of stupidity, but I've already mentioned the meathead's intelligence, or lack thereof. If they had egged or shaving creamed our cars or toilet papered our houses, we'd have laughed and admitted that we had it coming. Not only did the troglodyte get a felony conviction, one of our guys got so mad, he sugared the jock's gas tank.

The firecracker episode was the talk of the school and was recognized as the apogee of any stunt involving fireworks. Phil was really pissed off because he was a Benton and hadn't been invited. But he had one of his super bombs made up and ready to go.

That Friday, after I got off my job at the Forum Cafeteria, I went to the Alpha party that my friend, Donna, had invited me to. I wasn't much interested in Donna as a potential girlfriend, but Evelyn was an

Alpha and would be there so I wouldn't have missed it for anything. It was edging along toward midnight, I was dancing with Evelyn to the Platters and "Smoke Gets In You Eyes" (I would later perform it on electric bass with those very Platters). In walked Phil and my brother, Terry. I knew something was up, they looked like a couple of Bassett Hounds who had just crapped on the rug. Phil saunters over and says in a sub-tone, "If anybody asks, we were here all evening."

Saturday morning, I got up, poured a bowl full of Wheaties, splashed on the milk, and sat down to breakfast with the Kansas City Times. There, on the front page, was an article on how the Cliff Drive Spring had been destroyed by vandals the previous evening. I suddenly realized what the guilty looks were about, and I had no doubt in my mind as to who the vandals were. I

asked my brother about it and he said that he and Phil had been on a double date, and after they dropped the girls off, they took the customary high speed run around Cliff Drive. When they got to the spring, Phil had parked, gotten out of the car and walked over to the spring, lit a super bomb, put it in the basin and ran back to the Oldsmobile. Terry said he was horrified when the whole basin just collapsed.

It was the talk of the school that Monday. Now the neighborhood code was that you never talk to the cops about anything.

That is a peculiarity of poor neighborhoods - they don't like the cops. The attitude of the police toward teenagers, and Northeast in general, back then, had a lot to do with it. The police of today are very polite. (I no longer live in a poor neighborhood, anything but!) Back then it was always, "Where are you punks headed at this hour? Out of the car…Let's get a look in your trunk…" A neighborhood cliché was "He's a stand-up-guy". The definition of a stand-up-guy was, if you got caught, you took your medicine and didn't rat out your buddies, and if questioned about something, you never knew anything.

The spring incident was the talk of the school Monday. The heat had arrested Phil and held him for 72 hours, but they had to turn him loose when he wouldn't admit to anything. They didn't have any corroborating evidence and couldn't make a case. Terry got called down to the office and when he got there, there were two detectives waiting for him.

"Now Terry, we know you were there. We also know you didn't blow up the spring. We'll give you a complete pass, just tell us who did it. Now Terry had been there when a cop had slugged Bill McLaughlin over a little bit of nothing. When Bill's folks complained the two cops lied and denied the whole thing. It was common knowledge that they wouldn't hesitate to lie to you to get information that they wanted.

Terry, who was always testicularly well endowed, knew the meaning of the word, accomplice, and he wasn't about to incriminate himself.

"I don't know what the hell you're talking about."

"Well, I'll tell you what, punk, your ass is going to sit right here till you do," the cop snarled.

"That's fine with me. I don't want to go to friggin' class anyway."

They sat there about an hour, a Mexican stand off, with Terry giving them his best, most truculent glare. The cops couldn't rough him up because of the fact that Terry was a minor and the principal told them he couldn't let them talk to Terry unless he was present. They finally gave up and sent Terry back to class. Terry had gotten what he wanted. He had missed English. He always hated English.

The fuzz had not only figured out who the culprit was, they even knew who his running buddies were. Mr. Calvert, a well-liked chemistry teacher, had told them that Bob, a talented student, had shown an unusual interest in anything explosive. The newspaper article hadn't said that the spring was blown up, but merely "destroyed by vandals". They called Bob down to the office. Bob had read the article and spotted the trap. He walked into the office.

"What do you know about the Cliff Drive Spring incident?," that detective snapped, “You mean that spring that those guys busted up with sledge hammers?”

Next was Ron (not me). Ron was a Captain in the ROTC and he had his uniform on. He marched into the office and fired off a snappy salute, then stood at attention.

“What do you know about the Cliff Drive vandalism?”

Another salute, “Sir, nothing sir.” Ron said they kept repeating the questions and he kept saluting and saying, “Sir, nothing sir.”

This was the second time in less than a month we Bentons had initiated a shenanigan that had brought the police to Northeast High and, as a result, there was talk that the societies would be banned. They were, later, in 1962.

It was an open case for awhile but the entire student body of Northeast were “stand-up-
guys” and nobody ever spilled the beans. The cops knew what had transpired, but without a witness, their hands were tied. Phil was sullen’ surly, obstinate and alienated and they could have locked him up for a year and pounded his ass and he still wouldn’t have confessed.

The statute of limitations has long expired and I no longer feel any obligation to the neighborhood code. Over fifty years ago, Allan Phillip Harris blew up the Cliff Dr. Spring. Had not my brother been an inadvertent witness and had questionable culpability as an accomplice, I might have broken the code of silence back then. But Terry and I were tight, and we would have gone to the wall for each other. And had he thought he could have trusted the cops, he might have done the same thing, but experience had taught him that he couldn't.

They rebuilt the spring and it functioned for several years till someone got the bright idea to test the water. They were shocked to find trace elements of organic arsenic, so the spring was capped. Dumb old Phil had, through no good intentions on his part, done us all a favor. The alcove is still there.

After I graduated in 1960, I never had any desire to ever again belong to any social club, especially one that black-balled "undesirables", and I was in college for over ten years. (As a Benton, I had initiated a by-law that mandated we accept all applicants.) I had grown up and was glad to be leaving foolishness and sophomoric malarkey behind. The only organizations I joined after that were The Congress of Racial Equality, The American Federation of Musicians Local 34-627 and the Kansas City Bicycle Club.

Chapter 15 "Summer Olympics, 1960"

My friend, Tommy the goofball, was a great swimmer and never missed a chance to dive right in. The long hot summer of 1960, I had graduated from Northeast High and was working at the Forum Cafeteria as a baker's assistant. I was trying to save some money for college, but my '54 Chevy was going through it as fast as I could make it. I worked from 4 PM till 8:30 PM and my days off were Monday and Tuesday, which pretty much precluded a social life. By the time I got cleaned up from tending the ovens in the bakery, it was nine and too late to go on a date. I would usually hit one of the abundant "beatnik" coffee houses with my friend Ralph Earley, who worked my shift. Our favorite was 'Duke the Spook's" at 31st and Holmes where, as you entered, the first thing you saw was a planter made from a commode. Or I would join in on the poker game at Tommy the goofball's, or go cruising with the boys. We were all usually just a few cents from being flat broke so we had to be creative. There was always some resentment by my working class buddies toward the Southwest High School where all the money and privilege resided. When we went to the football games, we'd pull into the parking lot with our old junk heaps that we had worked to buy and park along side the shiny new convertibles that Daddy had bought for Junior. They were always arrogant and condescending. We resented being referred to as Northeast punks. We called them "cake eaters" or several other well known, often used phrases which in the interest of decorum, I won't repeat. There was resentment to the extent of acrimony, resulting in fights after football games. A misguided political statement is my theory.

I don't recall the specifics of how it began, but it was Tommy's idea, no doubt. It would start with a trip to Stanley's Tavern, on 7th Street in Kansas City, Kansas, where, if your voice had changed and you had a pulse, you could buy a couple of six packs at an exorbitant price, then proceed to the Southeast area where there was a plethora of private swimming pools. The idea of a private pool was so far beyond our reality that most of us had never even dreamed of one. The closest we would come would be the Boy's Club on Admiral Blvd. or the YMCA. We would wait till after 11 PM, when most people had retired, then cruise till we found a house with a pool. Then Tommy, Phil, Terry, Jim and whoever else was along, (we could squeeze 7 into Phil's step-dads big Oldsmobile,) would strip down to their skivvies, climb the fence, take off their skivvies, dive in the pool, swim down and back, then as the lights came on, put their skivvies back on then run like a cheetah chasing an Impala across the veldt, back to the car. I never was much of a swimmer, but loved cars and fancied myself as quite the high performance driver. The robin's egg blue Olds with the J-2 engine was a huge step up from my Chevy with the anemic six-banger. I would do almost anything to drive the Olds, so I usually went along as the wheel-man, pushing the accelerator to the floor , screeching the tires, as several wet teenagers piled in. My job was to be long gone by the time the cops showed up. The plan was to never repeat a performance in the same pool, and the goal was to hit every pool in the area by the time summer was over. We never got caught, but I'm sure if we had, we'd have been charged with only trespassing, the lowest of misdemeanors. Indecent exposure was never an issue because by the time the cops could have caught us, the guys would have had their junk tucked safely back in their blue jeans. The big thing was that it was free and that there was an element of risk to it and at, 17 or 18, I think every lad is an adrenaline junkie. We were confronting authority and thumbing out noses at the upper class and getting away with it. This activity went on for most of the summer.

The Concourse was a rectangular, meticulously maintained pool in the park at St. John and Benton, which was limited to the use of The Kansas City Casting Club for target casting with fishing rods. The Club had maybe 15 active participants on the best day. It had brightly colored hula-hoop like plastic rings as targets for the fat old guys who chomped cigars as they flicked their expensive rods, trying to center their lures in the rings. And no one else could use this pool in any way, whether the old fat guys and their cigars were there or not. There were "Absolutely No Swimming" signs posted on all four sides. We theorized that one of the casters was on the City Council. When we were 13, my buddy, Jim, bought a small electric motor called a "L'il Beaver" used for models and, having a terrific mechanical aptitude, quickly fashioned a clever model boat out of a sheet of balsa wood. It was powered by two D cell batteries. It ran quite well and our whole crew immediately wanted one. Being bereft of Jim's gift with machines (Let's face it, I had difficulty with complicated machinery like door knobs and zippers) I went to the Northeast Toy and Hobby shop and bought a model of a Johnson outboard motor and a speedboat kit with my earnings from my new job at Agron's market. Soon we all had battery powered model boats and were hanging out at the Concourse. We were treated with condescension and rudeness and were run out of the park with threats of police action. Nobody could do anything but cast there, no wading, no swimming, you couldn't even dangle your feet. Most of the time it stood vacant, waiting for a caster or two to show up, pristinely maintained at considerable expense by the city. This was regarded as elitist balderdash by most of the residents, but anytime an iconoclastic youth breached the protocol, the police were there in short order, and we always lost. Jim, being something of a contrarian, and angry over the inequity of the situation, fashioned a huge model sailboat out of a 2 by 8 plank which he called the "Sultana". It had two masts made of arrow shafts, a jib and sails made from discarded bed sheets, and a keel he had made by melting lead sinkers and pouring them into a mold.

One night he deliberately sailed it right into the middle of where the casters were smoking and practicing and a dispute ensued. One of the casters tried to snag it by casting his lure just over it and yanking back, but all he did was get his line tangled up in the rigging. Jim got a large stick and retrieved the Sultana, took out his pocket knife and cut the line which exacerbated the problem. The heat came and told us we couldn't sail our boats while the old smokers were casting.

After one of our swimming pool runs, we were hanging out, (loitering in police

nomenclature) at the Concourse. Tommy boldly proclaimed that 50 cents said he could swim two laps of the sacrosanct Concourse underwater without surfacing for a breath. Soon, half dollars were laid down and Tommy shed his clothes down to his birthday suit and hid them in the bushes. As luck would have it, Tommy no more hit the water when a police cruiser pulled up and stopped, and an officer got out and started walking toward us. Now like I said, people in poor neighborhoods don't feel warm and fuzzy when confronted with Kansas City's finest. You never called the cops. If you had a problem, you dealt with it yourself, and if it was more than you could handle you enlisted the help of your friends. When they pulled you over, and, if you were a teenager, they would pull you over, you answered their questions with as few words as possible.

"What are you doing out this late?"

"Driving."

"You think you're pretty smart?"

"Yes."

Terry was the master of smart-ass answers, which on occasion landed him in the tank. They never charged him with anything, they just ran him in and made Mom or Dad come get him. (At 69, he hasn't changed much.)

So when the cops showed up, we did what we always did, scattered in different directions so they could only run in one or two of us and not the whole bunch. We wouldn't give them the pleasure of seeing us run, but we walked, briskly, every man fending for himself.

The next weekend, we were all at Tommy's house for the poker game. He wasn't there, but he had left the basement door to the bar open so we could start without him. We were all there, smokes dangling from our mouths, trying to create a nonchalant, roguish countenance like James Garner in "Maverick". In stomped Tommy, as steamed as he could be.

"Which one of you motherfuckers stole my clothes the other night?"

We all swore that none of us had, or would, do that.

"I had to run six blocks home, naked as a fucking jaybird!"

We all cracked up at the thought of this which made Tommy even madder.

"I lost a brand new pair of Florsheims and my Mom keeps bugging me about where they are."

All of the participants in this particular adventure were present. Tommy said, "I'm going to ask each one of you who did this, and I want you to look me in the eye and give me a straight answer."

One by one, we testified with as much sincerity as we could muster. The simple fact was that all of us liked Tommy, he was in our crew, and none of us would have taken his clothes.

We all walked back up to The Concourse to look for his clothing, to no avail. There was neither clothing nor any clue as to its whereabouts. Tommy's Mom continued to rant about what had happened to his new loafers. "My god, Tommy, how on earth could you lose your shoes?"

We all pondered the deep mystery of Tommy's missing threads, and the answer became obvious. The flatfeet, seeing Tommy in the water and his clothes in the bush, picked them up and walked back to the cruiser and sat there laughing smugly as he ran home, soaking wet, buck naked for six blocks, down a well-lit Benton Boulevard, his bare ass glowing in the street lamp light. This had probably gotten lots of yuks at the police station. Once again, the cops had put one over on us Northeast punks.

Chapter 16 "Mr. Brown"

I stated early on my respect for teachers as an institution. Two of them greatly effected the arc of my life. I taught privately and at two colleges, the University of Missouri at Kansas City, and William Jewell college. I was an adjunct bass instructor at the former, and Director of Audio Recording at the latter, teaching a course in recording technology which I authored. I always thought that my job was to dispense accurate information, and when asked, to give well thought out advice with the student's best interest as the only concern, and above all, give every student my best, regardless of aptitude, favoring neither the gifted, nor giving the untalented so much of my time that I short changed everyone else. Some will fall by the wayside in spite of everything. Education is, after all, a weeding out process, separating the wheat from the chaff. But students who ultimately fail, should do so on their own and not be lifted by the scruff of their neck and thrown overboard. The last thing the podium should be is a venue for grandstanding or indulging in vanity. If there is anything sacrosanct, it should be that it's a process that is of and about the student, not the teacher.

I had two great teachers at old Northeast High, Harry J. Bianco for orchestra and Cossette Davis for English. Both were a life long inspiration. I also had some real duds. One, a biology teacher was the quintessential geek, who looked like the television character "Mr. Peepers". It was obvious that he really didn't like kids, but he didn't have the intellectual collateral to bag a college job. His mission seemed to be a mean-spirited pay back, one student at a time, for the genetic hand that he'd been dealt. After I graduated, "Geek" stepped so far over the line that one student beat him up after class. If I hadn't had good self control and not wanted to take any action that would jeopardize my future, that student could have been me. It was that bad.

The one who was most disappointing, however, was Mr. Brown, because he had so much potential. Teachers like "Geek" aren't that bright, they struggle through and get a job at a school that is not the gem of the district, and then it's get even time, or they go through the motions waiting for retirement. (I am still amazed at education's unwillingness to clean its own house.) Mr. Brown, however, was abundantly intelligent. He had the capacity to have been a great teacher, but his ego, personality and life-style got in the way. The idea of a high school *prima donna* has always seemed ridiculous to me. High school is the bullpen of life. But if ever there was a high school *diva*, it was Mr. Brown. He was extremely good looking, like James Dean, but in a more sophisticated less aggressive way, and was fresh out of the Ivy League. He looked and dressed like a model, which was way beyond his means. He wore only the expensive Hathaway shirts with the white collars and contrasting pastel bodies, which were sold only at Jack Henry's. He had one of every hue in the spectrum. (My friend, C. B., was a real clothes horse and knew not only where every item came from, but how much it cost to the penny.) His sport coats were all English tweed with suede patches on the elbows. His shoes were several different two color combinations of Ivy League saddle oxfords. (My personal sartorial adventures were limited to Sears.) C. B. calculated that Mr. Brown was spending more than he was making. His medium brown hair was always perfectly combed. He drove a neat little red '57 MGA that was always parked in the much desired first spot behind the "No Parking" sign in front of the school. He must have arrived at 6 AM to pull that off. Every student with a flashy ride wanted that slot, but Mr. Brown had it every day. All the best cars, George's heavily customized bronze '57 Chevy, Donnie's green '56 Ford convertible, Gary's turquoise '57 Chevy convertible and the other cool cars were all lined up for about a half block in pretty much the same order every day, but Mr. Brown's MG was always first.

I first started hearing about Mr. Brown in 1958, my sophomore year. My friend, Joyce, who was a year older than me, exuded intelligence and was something of a mentor to me, was always talking about him. Joyce's father was the Minister of Eastminster Presbyterian Church, so I saw her every Sunday. She was always talking about something Mr. Brown had said, regarding philosophy or some writer. Joyce was not only intellectually gifted, she was very competitive. She graduated at the top of her class and she seemed to be in a friendly intellectual jousting match with Mr. Brown. All the girls were swooning, sighing how dreamy he was, vying to sit on the front row so he would notice them - but Joyce was intrigued with his intellect. Most of the (straight) guys thought he was a pretentious poseur - a condescending, effete fop. I tended to agree with the guys, but never having had much contact with him, it wasn't a strong opinion.

Then a surprising development occurred. A group of friends and I frequented the Riverside stadium where, every Saturday night, the dirt track jalopy races were held. Riverside was a blue collar community, west of Kansas City, along the Missouri River, famous for the Red X cut rate liquor store and flooding every time there was a significant rain. It was gasoline alley, a Budweiser, baseball cap, tee-shirt kind of place, and the last place one would expect to see genteel, elegant Mr. Brown. He dressed down, in khakis and a sweat shirt with his omnipresent saddle oxfords.

The "stadium" consisted of a dilapidated ticket booth, a run-down refreshment stand, that had anything you wanted, as long as what you wanted was a hot dog, a hamburger or a carbonated beverage. The track was a high-banked eighth of a mile oval dirt speedway in front of weather beaten wood benches with no backs, behind a high chicken-wire fence to keep patrons from being pelted by the mud pellets the cars propelled at great speed as they roared out of the corners. The men's room was a very informal, antiquated affair featuring a urinal that consisted of a long metal trough with running water with no booths of any kind, where you walked up, whipped it out and took care of business, always looking straight ahead. No guy ever wanted to appear to be checking out another guy's apparatus. I had no interest in this topic whatsoever.

After relieving myself between races, I walked out and who should I see standing in the corner, where he had a full panoramic view of the whole row of peckers, was Mr. Brown. (He was there every week.) It was at that very moment that I knew Mr. Brown was gay. (This was later confirmed by several good looking classmates he had propositioned.)

In all my years of teaching, I had one absolute - any social contact with a student that had the least remote potential for sex was out -

no exceptions! One needed to avoid even the appearance of impropriety. Romantic involvement to me seemed to be the ultimate betrayal. We were there for their education and to guide them in early, critical choices that would impact the rest of their lives and that didn't include an extra curricular course in pubic relations. Though I had some offers, I always declined emphatically. I never even dated a student.

That fall, school started. Try as I might, I couldn't garner any enthusiasm. Who should I have for English, but Mr. Brown. I took a seat close to one of my Eastminster friends, Fanny, who was cuter than a cashmere sweater. Fanny never got into any trouble. Sitting next to her was her boyfriend, Richie, who was a real Adonis and a football player. Richie was Mr. Brown's favorite and got asked all the easy questions and Mr. Brown never challenged him or made him elucidate or defend his position like he did all of the rest of us. The opposite was true for Fanny who got all the tough questions, had to explain every answer in minute detail and if it didn't meet Mr. Brown's standards, he did his best to embarrass her. Fanny, though not intellectual in nature, was not stupid! She countered each of these Brown beachheads with increasing combativeness. I, by design, managed to stay clear of Mr. Brown's abundant and carefully laid land mines. Both my parents had been poverty driven high school dropouts who worked hard grasping for their share of the great American dream. Anything I'd learned of art or culture up to that point had been entirely on my own hook, and at that juncture of my life, wasn't much. My parents were completely occupied with just making a living. With my sixteen your old level of sophistication and life's experiences, taking on Mr. Brown was tantamount to spitting in Rocky Marciano's eye. I was out of my league at that point and knew it. (Five years later, he'd have needed to bring his lunch!) The last thing I wanted to do was stumble over one of Mr. Brown's clever trip-wires and embarrass myself. I didn't care what he thought of me. At sixteen, my professional music career had already begun and I knew what my life was to be and he had no power over that. I also knew that I was easily bright enough to get a C in any class at any time, which would get me where I wanted to be, out of boring high school and into the music business, so Mr. Brown had no axe to hang over my head. Becoming an academic was never part of my plan.

Then one morning Mr. Brown came in outraged. The actress, Debbie Reynolds, had made an appearance on "The Tonight Show" with host Jack Paar. Mr. Brown loved Jack Paar and frequently used Paar's catch phrase, "I kid you not". It appeared that Ms. Reynolds was just a bit into her cups and had attempted to disrobe Mr. Paar. Mr. Brown was outraged by this act of moral turpitude and launched a 20 minute diatribe on this transgression. I just sat there and shook my head in amazement. He thought his opinions were so profound and that he had the bully pulpit and could discuss whatever he wanted, whenever he wanted, even if it wasn't in the same zip code as the required curriculum.

Shortly after that, I arrived at school and in the revered first parking spot was the car that every teenager dreamed of, a brilliant new crimson Corvette convertible that had been a birthday present for a wealthy, very well-liked student, Tom, whose family were bankers. Right behind this paragon was Mr. Brown's MG, very pale in comparison. I hustled into class and took my seat. Mr. Brown, with his usual air of smug superiority, launched into a half hour fury about how the students' allowance was more than the teachers' salary. This was patently ridiculous. Tom was an anomaly, one of a very few rich kids. I had friends that were so poor, that they took ROTC because they needed the free clothes. Shortly after that, Mr. Brown threw in the vehicular towel and traded his MG on the lowest species of transportation, a mud-brown Renault Dauphine, a conveyance so low that no real car-person would be caught dead in it even as a passenger, let alone drive. They'd have preferred to walk. Mr. Brown made no further attempts to contest the coveted first spot, which now belonged to Tom by divine right. Mr. Brown now parked way back in the queue, down by the playground.

Representing himself as a musician and a jazz expert, Mr. Brown, who at one point, had played trumpet, convinced Mr. Bianco to let him lecture the Orchestra class one day. His knowledge of jazz and music in general was very superficial. He liked the dance bands like the Elgart brothers, Les and Larry. I already knew way more than he did on this topic and using his tactic, I asked him where he placed Gil Evans in the big band spectrum. He looked confused and sloughed off the question. It was obvious he didn't even know who Gil Evans was.

We were all required to pick a philosophy to do an oral report on. These were particularly lethal. Mr. Brown always turned these into a debate, which he invariably won, both on content and style points, using his rapier to carve up unsophisticated, working-class high school kids. Literature and poetry weren't that important to a kid whose Dad worked at the Ford plant. Most of us would become policemen, firemen, nurses, work at automobile assembly plants, sales clerks or in some instances, become part of organized crime. The upper-crust Pembroke Country Day School, where arrogance was regarded as a virtue, was where Mr. Brown should have been. I chose for my oral report, Humanism, because, having abandoned religion, it was the closest to home. Also, I had Joyce's excellent notes on her A report the previous year. I tore into it and worked really hard. I did my oral report, something that I did well at in college, and stressed that Humanism was a celebration of the collective creative accomplishments of mankind, and that, as an aspiring artist, I wished to find my place in that flow. I wrapped it up and quickly started to sit down. No one ever got off that easy.

"Mr. Roberts" (Mr. Brown was the only high school teacher who called his students by their last names, prefaced by Mr. or Miss. The gym teachers called us by our last names but without dignifying us with a Mr. I was just "Roberts".) (It was obvious to all that Mr. Brown thought a man of his prodigious talent should be a college professor.) "I consider myself to be both a Christian and a Humanist. Do you consider them to be mutually exclusive?", Mr. Brown challenged.

I immediately saw, right in front of me, a well placed booby trap designed to shed my blood, and I danced around it. Determined not to become Mr. Brown's daily serving of dog meat, I replied tersely - "I'd say that is a breach of logic, and as such, is your problem and not mine," and sat down. I caught him off guard and the class chuckled as he looked miffed. I had gotten a high, inside fastball by him. (I regarded any discussion of religion in high school as *verboten*. I had gotten a B in Civics and knew about the "separation of church and state" and since the school was part of the city school system, it was, thus, “state”.)

Fanny’s time was right after mine. She was at an even greater disadvantage than usual because Mr. Brown was already irked over my having quickly parried his thrust. Fanny, one of the Nor’easters who would become a registered nurse, did okay. Philosophy was not her strong suit. She finished and, like me, tried to make a quick getaway back to her seat, in vain. Mr. Brown tore into her like a pit bull on a pork chop. Having politely endured Mr. Brown’s affronts for months, Mt. Fanny erupted.

“I don’t really care and I’m damned tired of you picking on me all the time.”

The class was stunned. Fanny had said the “D” word. Richie, Fanny’s beau, was really steamed.

“Maybe you should just go on down to the office,” was Mr. Brown’s curt reply.

“That’s fine with me” Fanny spat out as she grabbed her books and exited in a huff, with her blonde pony-tail swinging defiantly.

Having someone stand up to him twice in one day kind of deflated old Brown for a while. Fanny got a couple of eighth hours for profanity.

But like I said earlier, Richie was on the football team, and this affair had yet to run its course. Shortly after that, I left school and started the walk home to my job at Agron's Market, and there, right before my eyes, was Mr. Brown's mud brown Renault sitting on the grass, resting between two trees with about an inch of wiggle room in the front and the back. Not even the great Roger Ward could have driven that car out of there. Rumor had it that the offensive line had, one on each corner, hoisted it and carefully placed it between two trees that were identical distance apart as the length of a Renault Dauphine. It would take either a hoist, or four guys of equal strength, not readily available, to extricate it. This had not been a spur of the moment stunt. They had to lie in wait, licking their chops, waiting for Mr. Brown to park his car within hauling distance of those two particular trees. They may have been strong enough to hoist it up over the curb, but they surely couldn't have carried it a half a block.

A crowd gathered with everyone laughing. Mr. Brown arrived in time to see a policeman writing him a ticket for illegal parking. Brown protested loudly, but to no avail. The car was, after all, on the grass, and it was his. I didn't want to be late for work, so I don't know what lengths they had to go to liberate the Renault, but I highly suspect that it was without assistance from the football team.

The year dragged on with Mr. Brown sometimes acting out all

the parts of a Shakespeare play, launching into his tirades at the slightest provocation. The day that his *alma mater* lost a football game to Syracuse University by 60 points, he came into class without saying a word and gave a pop quiz that almost everyone flunked.

The next year I had Miss Davis for English and she gave me the gift of Hemingway, Steinbeck, Salinger, and so many others. Literature became of staple in my life. I not only became a voracious reader, I married an excellent English teacher, who had a Master's degree plus many hours toward a specialist degree when she died. She had had Mr. Brown for English and felt exactly the same way I did about him. Miss Davis was delightful. Her song was always, "Isn't this wonderful!" Mr. Brown's riff was always, "Aren't I marvelous".

Chapter 17 "The Great Estes Park Cheesecake Caper of 1961"

The summer of 1960, my family vacationed in Los Angeles, making the trip in a new Nash Rambler station wagon that my Dad had borrowed from the leasing company where he was employed. We traversed old Route 66 at the end of its glory days, before the completion of the interstate highway system. It is indelibly stamped on my memory with all the souvenir shops and picturesque small towns. You miss all this on the interstate. My Dad packed so much fishing gear, including a heavy outboard motor that he would find wasn't ocean worthy, that there was hardly room for us. The Rambler was so overloaded that it pegged the temperature gauge on every mountain incline and we'd have to stop and let the car cool down.

In spite of having a pronounced tendency toward seasickness, Dad was determined to go deep sea fishing. He never caught anything, however, because he was unable to coordinate fishing and hanging over the side, heaving. (He hadn't learned anything from his experiences on our Florida vacation in 1958.) When we reached Eastern New Mexico, a life long love affair began. I was struck with the rugged beauty of the red buttes, the high plains desert and the Sangre De Christos mountains. I begged my Dad to stop for a day so we could try climbing, but he refused. He was anxious to get started with his fishing and puking. I figured my time was coming and made myself a promise that I would get back to the mountains at the first opportunity and go climbing.

It came sooner than I had expected. That winter, at mid-term of my first year of college at Kansas City Junior College, I was bereft of cash and if I wanted any social life at all, I would need a part time job. My Dad had advanced from a struggling wannabe to a successful salesman and was making big money, all of which he spent, every last cent. He didn't just have every expensive fishing device, he had at least two more in reserve. None of the money ever trickled down to me. I perused the college bulletin board for employment opportunities and was intrigued by an ad for the Estes Park YMCA of the Rockies stating that they would be hiring 75 boys and 175 girls for the coming summer. Man, I liked those odds. I promptly wrote for an application, filled it out and was delighted when the letter informing me of my acceptance arrived. Dad immediately started making rules, (he was always big on rules). I couldn't take the car that I had worked and paid for, I had to save some money (something he never at any point in his life, could ever do. Any time I managed to save a little, he promptly borrowed it, frequently forgetting to pay it back.) I should try to gain a little weight, and would have to write to my Mom at least once a week (totally unnecessary). My Dad's mission in life was to be a pain in the ass at every opportunity - my house, my rules, blah, blah, blah… He pretty much succeeded.

I surveyed the list of items I would need for the summer and immediately began purchasing them, blue jeans, an army surplus foot locker, WWII GI combat boots for hiking and climbing, and a big stack of classic novels I wanted to read. Mountains, here I come. I got a train ticket and left for a Dad-free summer which I was sure would be full of adventure, beautiful scenery, mountain climbing, and with 175 girls, possible romance!

I arrived in Denver after an all-night train ride. Sleep was the best way to endure the flat, boring 450 miles of Western Kansas. I caught the Greyhound for the fascinating ride up to Boulder, the rendezvous point where we were to meet the Estes Park Y Camp bus for the final leg up to Estes Park. I had a couple of hours to kill so I walked around the beautiful University of Colorado campus, and then won a bunch of free games on the bus station pinball machine. Kids starting coming in one at a time. Then the yellow Y-Camp bus showed up and we all got aboard. There were a couple of cute girls and three athletic looking guys with flat-tops who I soon found out were all Hoosiers, from Ball State University. One, Sam, would become my roommate.

Another, Bill, a big, freckled, redhead in a tan leather jacket would become a good friend. The scenery was fabulous, pine and aspen forests stretching right up to timberline, just what I'd been hoping for. We arrived and were assembled for orientation. I was surprised to find that I would be required to work six days a week, instead of the usual five. One of the directors, Helen, stressed that there would be absolutely no consumption of alcohol, not a big thing with me. I was never a heavy drinker, not even in college. Next came the lecture on sex. Love was to be only happy hand holding affairs like Wrangler Bob and his paramour, the statuesque Donna, who were held up as the ideal we should all strive to emulate. No male employees would be allowed inside the women's quadrangle under any circumstances. Next came the curfews. If we came in past 11:30 PM, we had to sign in at the reception desk, and it was made obvious that that would be looked on with disdain. Then we were given our job assignments and shown to our quarters. It was to be a summer of sobriety, celibacy and going to bed early.

The dorms were a huge disappointment. They were primitive, stark, wood structures resembling those in the movie, "Stalag 17". The rooms had just enough room for two beds, a chest and a minute closet. There was one bathroom between each two bedrooms, meaning it would be shared by four guys. The heat vent was a rectangular hole sawed in the knotty pine wall up by the ceiling, (did these people not know that hot air rises?) and there was one bare light bulb screwed into a fixture in the wall. I began to get a very uneasy feeling about what I had gotten myself into for 60 bucks a month. Reality had kicked in. I wouldn't be spending much time in the dorm. The brochure they had sent hadn't pictured the dorms, but the fancier guest quarters and had stated we would receive room and board. Now I regard board as three square meals a day. I was amazed to find that they would not be providing dinner on Sunday evenings. Downtown Estes Park was too far to walk so our only options were one of their overpriced restaurants, the pricey, mediocre, sandwich shop, the expensive grocery store, or tough it out. The $60 a month went down to 50 right there.

The early issue was the food, which met with universal derision for both quality and

quantity. They must have studied at the Northeast High School Center For Culinary Disaster. There were never any fresh fruits or vegetables. It was a steady diet of mushy, overcooked spaghetti and such delicacies as cold longhorn cheese sandwiches. They made no concessions to body size. Two-hundred-fifty pound boys were served the same portions as one-hundred pound girls. The kitchen was run by "Big Jim", a retired hash-house owner from Brooklyn and his wife Bertha, aka "Boitha", who supervised salad and dessert preparation and stood at the end of the line in the employee's lunch room with her arms crossed and a sour milk scowl on her surly countenance. She was the kitchen "S.S." who made sure that no one went through the line twice and that no one took two of anything. My read was that she and Big Jim had a piece of the action. A friend, Ted, who was a guitarist and a scholarship football player at a small Texas college was very concerned about keeping his weight at 225 for his role as a linebacker in the coming football season. He was extremely annoyed at the small amount of food he was being served. One day he reached through and took four of the tiny cartons of milk they provided. As he reached for number four, Boitha reached through the steam trays and started to remove three of them. Ted snagged her wrist in a vice-like grip and met her scowl with one that would have scared a grizzly bear. Boitha refused to give in and a stand-off ensued for about five minutes, with neither yielding, blocking the line. Boitha, realizing that her position was untenable, and that the line was obstructed so that no one could eat and go to work, finally gave in. My Mom was a great cook in an American standards sort of way, and though, in my very early life, we had been quite poor, we always had plenty of good food and I always got as much as I wanted to eat. Though I was very slender in those days, I had a big man's appetite. I had the classic fast metabolism.

I was stunned to find that my work assignment was as a cook for "The Pine Room", their up-scale restaurant. While I had some food experience at the Forum, I had stated on my application that I had been a baker's assistant, not a cook. I had never cooked much of anything.

So much for the summer out-of-doors. We cooks were given instructions on how to operate the equipment and a timing chart for the deep fryer and the grill for steaks and chops. The menu had nothing with sauces or anything fancy. One would have thought that Big Jim would have stuck around for a week or so, to be sure that we got the hang of it, but this was not the case. We were issued hats and aprons and put right on the front line. None of the other kids had any more experience than I did, but they were an intelligent crew and tried hard. One guy, another Ron, I found particularly amusing. He was a voice music major and sang Broadway show tunes all the while he worked. Another fellow burnt off his eyebrows and all the hair off his arms trying to light the gas stove. Luckily, he wore glasses and had on one of the regulation hats, or it could have been a lot worse. The first week was a disaster. The waitresses weren't any more experienced than we were and got the orders all screwed up. It was high stress with everyone seeming to arrive at the same time, with confused waitresses yelling about their messed up orders and putting their tickets at the front of the wheel instead of the back making it impossible to fill the orders in the proper sequence. People who had been there for ten minutes got their food before folks who had been waiting for a half hour. The waitresses blamed all of their mistakes on us, but usually, the tickets vindicated us. We simply divided up the orders and each of us cooked what was on the ticket. We had a really angry clientele. I had worked at a well run restaurant with professionals and being a cook or a waitress is harder than people think. You have to do several things at once and keep them straight. I was amazed at how stupid they were to launch the season with a completely green crew.

Now I've always had a guerilla attitude. Maybe it came from, at that time, being 5' 11

and ¾ inches and weighing in at a whopping 128 pounds. A direct frontal assault was seldom the prudent move. Or maybe it comes from being part Native American. I was damned if I was going to spend the whole summer being hungry. I resolved the food situation on my own. Being a cook had its advantages. I'd just wait for the rush to be over, then cook as much of and

whatever I wanted and eat it on the back porch. Steak, shrimp, trout - I

have always believed in
being good to myself.

What I had gotten myself into was 48 hours a week of stress, on my feet, six days a week. Conversations with my friends confirmed I had gotten the worst of a bad lot. The pretty girls got the easy jobs as receptionists and clerks, sitting around all day. The less attractive girls were maids, working their tails off. I soon figured out why we had had to send pictures with our applications. There wasn't much to do there outside of work. They had an abundance of activities, horse back riding, crafts, tours, but if we wanted to participate, we had to pay like the guests. There was an employee's recreation hall that had a television and a record player, but since no one wanted to spend any time in the dorms, it was always packed to capacity. If we wanted to go to downtown Estes, those of us without cars had to hitch a ride with another employee or borrow a car. Both entailed buying gas, something I could ill afford. There was a free bus a few times a day, but it didn't run at night when most of us had free time. It was obvious I wasn't going to be saving any money. I thought about splitting, but decided to stay and make the best of it. I managed to get in a little climbing on my days off.

I was surrounded by Hoosier frat-boys. Nearly everyone in my building was from Indiana and a Tau Kappa Epsilon, or Teek. My roommate was a Ball State jock, Sam, who had developed an insatiable fondness for Coors beer, which in those days was not available in the eastern half of the country. His love of loose women was already well in place, in spite of a picture on his dresser of an attractive young lady whom he had given his fraternity pin. He described himself as engaged to be engaged. He soon found an enthusiastic co-conspirator named Mary who shared both of his vices. He cleverly found an old stone building with a fireplace about a half mile from the camp, that had fallen into disuse, which became a private place where he could pursue his twin interests. This, however, was short lived. Some of the other horny, boozing frat boys were just as clever as Sam and soon the old house was packed. The powers-that-be had to understand that hiring 250 college kids would include a percentage of drinking, carousing frat boys and my roomy was the prototype. I mentioned the light bulb protruding out of the wall, bereft of a shade or covering of any sort. It was our habit to leave it turned on. Estes was 7000 feet in elevation, and no matter how warm the day had been, the temperature really plummeted at night. The heater was in the front of the structure and my room was at the rear - very little heat got back there. We usually left the bulb turned on to create a little warmth.

After about a month of mistakes by fledgling chefs, they finally gave up and hired a real cook from one of the other resorts. A few of us got transferred to dishwashing, which was a real break. They had commercial dishwashing machines and all we had to do was scrape the dishes, load the machines and then stack the clean dishes. We were each required to work two meals a day, or twelve meals a week. It involved less than being a cook and we didn't have the scrutiny of the ever glowering, ubiquitous Boitha, looking over our shoulders. Now I'm a man who has always recognized immediately when he was being taken advantage of, and I decided to level the playing field. Inspiration struck. I quickly figured out that if we worked three meals a day, we could fill our requirement in just four days, leaving three free to maybe take some side trips, view the spectacular Rockies, and do some overnight climbs. This met with universal approval and we implemented this plan. After about three weeks the management figured out what we were doing and told us to cease this insurrection. Everybody had to work six days, period. To enforce this, we were required to submit our weekly schedule for approval. We simply turned in a phony schedule and had three days off for the rest of the summer. The four days were hard, ten hour days, but it was worth it for three days of freedom.

One of the musicians I had befriended, Mark, a flautist, was dating one of the pretty girls who had a desk job in the office. She had told him that Alan, whom everyone called "Camel", because he never went anywhere without his canteen affixed to his belt, was the camp stool pigeon, (like Peter Graves in "Stalag 17"). She said that he made daily trips to the office to rat out any of us who had strayed, ever so slightly, from the prescribed straight and narrow path, and was encouraged to do so. That information was soon all over the Y-Camp and Alan became *persona non grata*. Mark was also a big practical joker. One of the guys in our billet, shunned bathing in any form and also avoided washing his clothing. Mark lived next door to "Stinky" and was fed up with the rank odor engulfing the whole building. He constructed a clever device he called a "Babo Bomb". While the olfactory offender was at work, Mark put a swimmer's clip on his nose and went into Stinky's room. He removed the light bulb from the wall socket and cracked and removed the glass, being careful not to damage the filament. He then taped a firecracker to the naked filament and, using masking tape, he attached the "bomb", a can of cleanser mixed with cocoa, that had the end cut out of it to clear the filament, and screwed the contraption back into the wall socket. When Stinky can home and turned on the light, the hot filament ignited the firecracker fuse, which then exploded and blew cleanser and cocoa everywhere. Then he and a couple of other guys who had waited for Stinky to come home, after the explosion, stormed his room and manhandled him into the shower, fully clothed, turned on the water and then doused him with shampoo. They wouldn't let him out for ten minutes. Stinky got the message and implemented a program of personal hygiene.

All of us musicians soon found each other. We always do. Monday night jam sessions became a joy. One day I got a message saying that I should come to the Program Director's office at my first convenience. I went there after my shift and was told that Sarah, a good singer whom I had met at the jam sessions, was going to be singing at the weekly steak cookouts. They were an extra cost option for the guests. I was told, not asked, that I would be accompanying her.

I thought for a moment, then replied I was a professional musician and had been such since the age of fifteen. I pointed out to him that I was already working nearly fifty hours a week, which fulfilled any contractual obligations I had to the Y-Camp. While I performed for free at employee parties and social functions, if I were to play at an event where tickets were being sold, I would need some compensation. He replied, emphatically, that that wasn't in the cards. I told him that I wasn't going to work more than fifty hours a week, but I would be happy to play if he reduced my dish washing responsibilities by one meal a week. He said he would get someone else. Either Sarah didn't want someone else, or there wasn't anyone else that could, who would do it. He called me and said that the cookouts were on Wednesday and that I would be excused from the Wednesday evening meal. The head dishwasher, Keith, had been given the position by virtue of the fact that he had arrived a couple of days before everyone else. He was a big sandy haired klutz of a drunken frat-boy who told tasteless, racist jokes and broke more dishes than anyone. He, on one occasion, had managed to drop a whole stack. Every shirt he owned had Tau Kappa Epsilon emblazoned on it except the one that depicted a little cartoon man sitting on many cases of beer. A cartoon balloon said, "72 cases of beer and not one damn church key" (fifties slang for beer openers. Aluminum pop-top cans hadn't been invented yet. This two headed device had a square end with a bottle cap remover and a pointed sharp end for puncturing holes in tin beer cans. Without a "church key" tin beer cans couldn't be opened.) Management had forbidden him to wear that shirt, so he wore it inside-out. When I informed him that I would be working the Wednesday cook-outs and was now responsible for only 11 meals a week, he exploded into a profanity laced tirade. (Profanity of any kind was also a big "no".) He said I would no longer be eligible for the three meals a day program. My retort was that in view of the this, I was no longer eligible to trek up the hill when he didn't show up for his breakfast shift, pound on his door till he awoke from his drunken stupor, inform him of his responsibility to the rest of us, watch him stagger out of bed smelling like a bar towel, looking like he was bleeding to death through the eyeballs, and walk him down the hill. If I left, he would just go back to sleep. I informed him that the rest of the dishwashers were good kids who worked hard and we were tired of carrying his lazy ass. I concluded with the next time this was an issue, I'd just let Big Jim handle it. The only thing that had saved his worthless ass, so far, was my adherence to the tough neighborhood code of never ratting anybody out, and he was no longer eligible for that program. He was much bigger than me and it was obvious he wanted to punch me, but that would have resulted in immediate termination. I was subsequently reinstated in the 3 days off format. Of all the people they could have chosen, they had picked the biggest loser in camp!

The first cookout came and Sarah and I were a huge success. She was cute, perky, and had a wonderful, clear soprano voice, perfect for the folk music that was so big in 1961. As the evening drew to a close, Sarah and I were stunned that we wouldn't be allowed to eat. As we had missed the dinner hour in the employees cafeteria, that meant a bowl of cold cereal for dinner, not a pleasing prospect. Religious organizations always seem to be like that. When they stick it to you, they're like the Bob Dylan song, they've got "God On Their Side". I was furious and was waiting for the Program Director when he got to his office the next morning. I told him, bluntly, that Sarah and I were highly offended by the shabby way we'd been treated after performing for two hours. If working the cookouts entailed watching people eat broiled sirloin, while we missed our dinner hour and had to eat Wheaties for supper, he had seen our final performance. He looked confused, then asked why Big Jim hadn't taken care of us. I informed him that Big Jim considered taking care of us, handing us a little box of Wheaties and a carton of milk, and had heretofore, never gone beyond that. I also asked him if he'd eaten in the employees cafeteria lately? He looked quite put out and consented to feeding Sarah and me. Every Wednesday it was sirloin, a backed potato, Indian corn cooked on the broiler with the green shuck on it, and apple pie. Blessed are the loud of mouth for they shall receive. (Keith would have been so mad he'd have had an aneurism if he'd known I was getting steak.)

A few nights later, I was asleep, when I smelled something burning. I leaped up and soon found the source of the smoke. My roommate, Sam, had staggered in way past the curfew as was his habit, removed his trousers before retiring, and hung them on the light bulb, which was turned on for the heat. I quickly analyzed the situation and decided the intelligent course of action was to remove said trousers from the light bulb and take them in the bathroom and douse them in the sink to extinguish the embers. That morning, Sam woke up with the mother of all hangovers, and asked me why his khakis were wet. I pointed to the burn mark and told him how it had got there, and having no desire to perish in a fire, (the tinder box we lived in would have gone up like a matchstick,) that he should either dial back his Coors consumption, or make other living arrangements. Then all hell broke loose. It seemed that Sam and Mary had spent the evening in a prominent Estes watering hole called “Jax Snax”, gotten completely loaded and staggered in about 2 AM. It was their great misfortune that Camel had been on duty and they woke him up when performing the required sign-in. Camel did what he always did, raced to the administration the next morning to rat Sam out. Sam was called into the office and was told that there would be a hearing at which he would be informed that he was being sent home. Now, practically everyone there was over 18 , and thus no longer minors. They couldn’t send anyone home. All they could do was fire you. They had no control over what happened after that. Sam was a good looking bus-boy in the Pine Room, was funny, energetic, a good worker and very popular with the kitchen and Pine Room staff, especially the female portion. I was a Political Science major in those days and knew immediately what needed to be done. We drafted a resolution that stated that if Sam were dismissed, the entire kitchen and Pine Room staff would resign , *en masse,* effective immediately and the whole group signed it. It was strangely quiet around the camp. The next time I saw Camel, he had a huge shiner.

Mark kept us all laughing with his creative practical jokes. He managed to wire up the garbage truck in such a way that every time you applied the brakes, the horn honked. It took them nearly a week to figure out how to undo that one. Then he got a telephone repairman's hat and a ladder and climbed into the second floor of the girls quadrangle and released a gopher he had caught. Then he got caught in mid act. He had sunk a piton into the main dining hall chimney and was apprehended rappelling down the side of the structure.

I managed to have some fun, in spite of a lack of funds. A group of us piled into John's '57 Ford 8 passenger station wagon and went to the Cheyenne Frontier Days Rodeo. We got to see the great Casey Tibbs. The sleeping arrangements, the '57 Ford, left a lot to be desired. Six guys was about 3 too many. One of our fellow kitchen workers, a different Keith, had access to a family cabin with a wood stove in Fairplay, Colorado. Keith called in sick and four of us piled in his VW and went up there and climbed for three days.

Along towards the end of the summer came the high point, climbing Long's Peak, the highest mountain in the Rockies. I was really looking forward to this. It involved an 18 mile trip leaving at 2 AM to enable us to get off the peak before noon. In the Rockies, static electricity builds up in the afternoon to the point that walking between two rocks and shorting them out can cause quite a jolt. One guy suffered mild burns on his arms. The other consideration was that afternoon lightning was very prevalent and that standing at 14,256 feet, you were the tallest thing around. Becoming a potential lightning rod was not an appealing prospect. We hit the trail after stoking up on Wheaties and sweet rolls we found in the kitchen which wasn't open till 8 A.M., and picking up our sack lunches we had ordered ahead. (If you were going on an all day hike, you could order a sack lunch which meant you weren't eligible to go through the cafeteria line. Boitha stood at the end of the line with a list. Heaven forbid that they feed someone twice.) The early part was just hiking, but constantly upward. The rise would be over 7,000'. We were young, in good shape and we made excellent time. This was possible till you hit the boulder field, an abundance of huge rocks that surrounded the base of the peak. They were in every direction, with no clear path. It was slow going, hopping from boulder to boulder, or in some case, scurrying up and down them. Finally we hit the base of

Long's working our way slowly up the steep, rocky trail. We were way above timberline and at this point the altitude really takes its toll. After a couple of hours we came up to the cables. The National Park Service had sunk heavy screws into rock and attached two lengths of cable, approximately 30 feet each, to enable climbers to ascend the vertical surface. There are two ways up Long's, the Keyhole, or the cables, which is roughly two hours shorter. There were around twenty of us, so it took a while. Being pretty winded, we needed the rest. Then we went up the final stretch to the peak. There have been few things in life that have exceeded my expectations. This was one of them. It was too beautiful for words, but I'll try. Because of thousands of feet of less atmosphere, the sky is a deeper azure, with marshmallow clouds. We crossed a jade-green meadow where you could see what seemed like all the way to Kansas in one direction, and clear to California in the other. Muskrat-like creatures called conies and flightless birds named ptarmigans roamed in the meadow below. It was rapturous! Then, I did a dumb thing. I had a bet with a friend that I could smoke an L & M cigarette and stay conscious. (I quit smoking over forty years ago.) I won, but not by much. Then we sat down and unpacked our lunches. There was an orange, the first fresh fruit I had had all summer, a Hershey bar and a sandwich wrapped in wax paper. I unwrapped it and was disgusted to find the puniest peanut butter and jelly sandwich I had ever seen. The guy that had spread the peanut butter had almost missed. I expressed my outrage at high volume. These people treated food like it was platinum. Trixie, the hike leader, said that that was all they ever sent and that she had brought extra food, but she didn't offer any to me, but she did say she didn't eat chocolate and gave me her Hershey bar. The truth hit me like a bolt out of the blue. I had been conned. They had taken advantage of adventurous college kids, paid them practically nothing, significantly below federal minimum wage, underfed them, and charged the guests ridiculous prices. I had been working for around 20 cents an hour! Up to this point, I had spent two months honestly trying to live up to my end of the bargain. I now understood the rules. There weren't any but the old bottom line. What were we going to do about it anyway? We were stuck and they knew it. I vowed to do something and that would start with doing as little as possible for the remaining month. That is the instant in time that I developed my flexible ethic. Having had humble beginnings, I had, up to now, never been the one to make the rules. But I was clever enough to see what they were and we'd be playing from the same deck for what was left of the summer. My new code was that you get what you give and that has served me well in my forty-five year career in the music business which is rampant with bullshit. I made up my mind to do anything I could to square accounts, and that would begin with Boitha.

We started the descent. My stomach felt like my throat had been cut. We crossed a huge, tilted strata of rock which sloped to a thousand foot drop-off. It was quite intimidating. Trixie had given us strict instructions to walk at a right angle to the rock so that our weight would be on the tread of our hiking shoes for traction. She stressed that people who sat down and tried to scoot would soon be scrapped off the rocks 1000 feet below. We traversed that slanting rock very slowly. It emerged to a very narrow trail with a good view down the vertical face. We went through a rock formation know as "The Keyhole" and emerged, once again at the boulder field and began an uneventful, but hungry trek back to the Y-Camp. That little venture took over eighteen hours as I recall. I mooched a couple more Hershey bars along the way. A couple of the girls were on a diet and wouldn't eat sweets on a bet. We arrived at the trail head and the camp bus was waiting for us there. We rode back to the camp and twenty starving hikers who had missed dinner headed for the kitchen for some chow. If the cooks had had their way, I'm sure they would have accommodated us. But it was our hard luck the Boitha was on duty at the salad/desert stand. The edict was that the kitchen was closed and we were on our own. After serious sub-tone cursing, insulting her number of legal parents, her intelligence, and her lack of anything approaching human kindness, I had been a cook and remembered where they stored the cereal. We waited for her to leave and I cleaned out the cereal cabinet. One of the girls knew the combination to the lock on the refrigerator to get milk, and we finally had a dinner of sorts, the breakfast of champions.

That was the final insult and it was guerilla tactics from then till departure time. I began to devise schemes to take time off. Shortly after that, my Mom and Terry arrived. They had made reservations as soon as my employment had been confirmed. Mom was alarmed at the six pounds I had lost and asked "Don't they feed you?" "Only when it's convenient" was my terse reply. She gave me twenty bucks for food emergencies. Terry did what he always did in any situation, immediately found a girlfriend. I took my three days off and did some sightseeing with Mom and Terry. She insisted on buying me great lunches and dinners (Good ol' Mom!) Then I called in sick for the next three days. There was a gastrointestinal disorder that frequently effected people who weren't used to high altitude. It didn't always strike immediately, but lay, insidiously, in wait. Management's euphemism was "mountain madness". The usual effect was that you didn't want to stray too far from a toilet for six of seven days. I figured it was good for a week, so I made the trip to the infirmary, reported my "malady" and got the prerequisite bottle of Kaopectate. Next came dealing with Keith. I knew I needed some leverage. I was well aware of Keith's running all night drunken poker game, which was the reason for his inability to rise and perform his duties. I also knew from the guys that had lost money to him that Keith was something of a card shark. Gambling was very high up on the list of nos! I called Keith in the kitchen and told him that I was ailing and unable to work, then held the phone away from my ear to avoid the high volume tirade that I knew would ensue. Then I asked him how much he had won last night. This stopped him in his tracks. I pointed out that there were some people that were very unhappy over their losses and it would be very simple to connect the dots, and if he intended to stay for the rest of the summer, he would be well advised to shut the fuck up and cover for me. That turned the trick. I spent three more days hanging with Mom and Terry.

Then I got a break from an unexpected source. My friend Bill, the big red haired Hoosier I had befriended on the way in, who had weighed 220 pounds, was down to 200 and suffering from a severe case of the hives. Bill was a stock boy for the kitchen and had a very early morning, pre-breakfast shift, which left him free to pursue his primary interest, coeds. He was quite good looking and extremely charming, so in short order, he had an afternoon girlfriend

who worked the night shift, and an evening girlfriend who worked the day shift. Neither knew of the other. The combination of several factors, he had two dates everyday and was staying out till one or so every night, then getting up At 5:30 AM to be on the job at six, the poor diet and the altitude had hit him with a triple whammy. He was in rough shape. The nurse had become very concerned about him and suggested that he be given a few days off and sent to Denver to see a doctor. They consented to giving him time off toward that end. Bill, always the rascal, immediately stated that he didn't feel strong enough to make the trip by himself, that he needed a back up. They said he could take one person. He picked me and I was assigned to be his traveling companion. I told Keith of my assignment, which met with the usual overreaction. He had used his position to do nearly nothing for the first couple of months and I confess to having a bit of a mean streak where bullshitting phonies are concerned. I enjoyed seeing him have to cover my shift. I informed him that I had been given an assignment by the administration and had no say in the matter, and if he was unhappy with their decision, he could discuss it with them. I also said I hoped he'd use the same adjectives he'd thrown my way. (Keith really wanted to kick my ass, but he knew if he did, then Bill would really pulverize him, and Bill knew how.)

We got a ride on Thursday with a fellow employee who was going to Denver on his day off. Bill's instructions were to see a doctor on Friday and return Friday evening. We could stay at the Denver YMCA for free because we were Y employees. Now Denver is 2,000 feet closer to sea level than Estes Park. Bill's condition was legitimate, but the altitude decrease made for immediate, significant improvement. It was like a turbo-charger had kicked in and he was suddenly full of energy. He said he had a great idea, that he'd call the Y-Camp and tell them that he couldn't get in to see a doctor till Monday, and that we would return that evening. He pulled it off and we were free for a weekend on the town in Denver. I still had the $20 Mom had given me and, in the days of 35 cent draw beer, that would go a long way. We wandered around and did some sightseeing, found an inexpensive cafeteria with great food, where we really pigged out, and that evening we found a wonderful night club that featured a terrific African/American folk singer named Don Crawford. They also had 35 cent Lucky Lager dark beer on draft. Bill and I spent Friday and Saturday there. Monday, Bill did succeed in getting an appointment with a physician who told him what we all already knew, it was a combination of altitude and burning his candle at both ends. He gave Bill some medication for his hives. Bill said he had called around and rounded us up a ride for that night. I had a good dinner with the last of the $20 Mom had given me (I hadn't spent it all on beer, I did buy some food.) We walked back to the Y and waited for our ride, and who should show up but Keith. He was really pissed and said he wasn't

taking me anywhere. Bill could be very persuasive, and still had 200 pounds of muscle left. Keith weighed that much, but it was all beer fat. Bill won the argument. Keith's car was a Nash Metropolitan, a sub-compact with a back seat suited only for newborn babies and circus midgets.

I was shoe-horned into this abomination along side 6'4" Bill. Keith, always as disagreeable as possible, and sensing my discomfort, rolled down the window on the soon to be 40 degree night, and drove as slowly as the law allowed. Just when you think things can't get any worse, they invariably do. Bill was having one of the greatest gas attacks of all times. It smelled like a feeding lot! I have never known a human who was capable of producing that much methane, except my step-son Eric, who not only has an amazing volume of flatulence, but can issue it on command. That was the longest ride of my life. I suffered no major olfactory damage, but my right knee seemed to be misaligned for a couple of days.

The next day I decided I had more comp time coming, I was only half way through the big stack of books I had brought, and I needed to get to the Dostoyevsky and Faulkner. I called Keith, who shouted a dumbfounding stream of expletives, none of which were repeated, at a terrific amplitude. I think he broke the Guinness record for non-repetitive cussing. He complained that I had just had a week off and had spent the week-end in Denver. I countered with the weekend in Denver had been a working assignment to aid an ailing colleague. I then appropriated Bill's gastrointestinal distress (his farting had been omnidirectional) and asked Keith if he was devoid of a sense of smell, or was just being obtuse? I told him I had seen a doctor in Denver about the "Mountain Madness" and he had said that I should take it extremely easy for a few more days. I then pointed out, accurately, that he had worked fewer hours than any other dishwasher, by a long shot, and that the poker game would have to wait and he'd have to just suck it up.

Shortly after that, a group of friends and I were sitting around, bemoaning the fact that it

was two more weeks till payday and we were all broke as usual. One of the fellows, John, had taken a trip from New Haven, where he went to Princeton, to New York and had seen the great Bertolt Brecht/Kurt Weill play, "The Threepenny Opera." He suggested we should have a beggar's banquet, like in the play, where everything had to be stolen. This suggestion met with immediate, unanimous, enthusiastic approval. Bill, as the kitchen stock boy, volunteered to purloin a couple of cases of soft drinks. Jim, who was a clerk in the grocery store, indicated that snack cakes, chips and dip wouldn't be a problem. If we would come in, one at a time, and take what we needed, he'd gladly be looking in the other direction. One of the cooks said he'd nail several packages of wieners, and we could go down to the old house, build a fire and cook them on sticks in the fireplace. The idea snowballed and started its trip down the mountain. I wondered what, as a dishwasher, I could contribute, then inspiration struck. I could land a shot on Boitha's always sour kisser, and serve the party at the same time. Boitha considered her cheesecake to be her masterpiece. She was so proud and protective of it that it was under heavy security, and whenever she left the kitchen, it was placed in the walk-in refrigerator and the door was locked. (I've eaten cheesecake at the world famous Stage Delicatessen in New York City and I can attest to the fact that Boitha suffered from illusions of cheesecake grandeur. Her's was so far under that at the Stage, that it was not worthy of being mentioned in the same chapter.) I began to concoct a scheme to execute this maneuver. I remembered that Melissa, a girl I had dated a couple of times, who worked in the salad/dessert area, despised Boitha. I told her I needed a cheesecake and that her end of the deal would be a slice and an invitation to the party. She laughed and said that what she could do was to "forget" to put one in the cooler and if it got snatched off the counter, well so be it. She came through and I embarked on a short-lived crime spree. I filched the cheesecake just before my shift ended and wrapped it in my jacket as I walked up the hill. It was a cool rainy day, and the temperature in my room was usually the same as that outdoors, so there wasn't any danger of spoilage. The party was set for later that evening.

The hot dogs were cooked and eaten, the cokes drunk, the cheesecake consumed…the soiree was a smashing success at no cost to the participants. Everyone in attendance had been sworn to absolute secrecy.

The next day the grand inquisition commenced. They did everything but call in J. Edgar Hoover. You'd have thought someone had cracked the safe and stolen the month's payroll. One by one the kitchen workers were called into the kitchen and asked about the disappearance of Boitha's precious cheesecake. The code of silence was maintained. The investigation continued on for about a week. No one, in spite of intense pressure, cracked. Management put out a little weekly newsletter (manipulative propaganda) called the "Peaker". The next issue came out and was devoted entirely to uncovering the unconscionable hooligan who had nabbed the cheesecake. It became the camp joke and every wannabe took credit for my fearless act and bragged that he/she had been the culprit.

I actually did return to work for the last couple of weeks, but only at a Keith-like pace. Then the big news hit. The winsome, shapely Donna had come up preggers! Evidently, she and Wrangler Bob had gotten beyond the happy, hand holding stage, and Bob had rounded third base and scored, and his seed had fallen on fertile ground. I felt completely inadequate. Wrangler Bob and Donna were the fine examples of Y-Camp virtue that everyone should follow, and I had not only not knocked anyone up, I hadn't even gotten laid. What at disappointment I must have been to Helen.

The whole misadventure ended with a September snow storm. At the closing of the

season, the accumulated tips that had been put into a common pool were supposed to be divided among the employees who had worked till the end. (Most of us felt that much of the tip money

had ended up in somebody's pocket and not the communal tip jar.) It was obvious that this policy was in place to keep disgruntled employees from jumping ship. Many ignored it and left anyway. It came time to return to Kansas City and I went to the administrative office to collect my last paycheck and my share of the tips. They gave me $41 and told me I was required to read my evaluation by my supervisor. Keith, the lush, had stated that I was lazy, unreliable and a troublemaker. I asked the lady if she had smelled Keith's breath when he turned in the report? She asked what did I mean by that? I replied that Keith had spent most of the summer in a drunken poker game and hadn't showed up enough to be entitled to an opinion. I then thought about hunting Keith, and despite my weight disadvantage, (I always had really fast hands) initiate a discussion with the potential for injuries, but quickly thought better of it. I didn't give a quark what any of them thought, and I would never, under any circumstances, list this debacle on my resume. I would be embarrassed for anyone to know that I had been that big of a sucker. I had worked away my whole summer vacation, mostly washing dishes, lost 10 pounds and it had cost me about $200.

When I got home, my Dad asked me how much money I had saved? I asked him how much he had saved? His retort was, "Do as I say, not as I do, blah, blah, blah, blah…"

My fascination with mountain climbing began in 1960 and ended in 1961. I had wanted to see what it looked like up there and Long's Peak scratched that itch. I never went climbing again. In 1962, a friend of mine, a wonderful guy, Gary Noland, had loved climbing so much, he had returned to work at the Y-Camp. He lost his life on one of the peaks that I had climbed.

Forty years later a friend introduced me to his sister, "She works in Estes Park". I told her I had worked at the Estes Park Y-Camp and she said that that was where she worked. I told her of my experiences and she quickly replied that nothing had changed. "They hire more kids than they need, they're not paying them much of anything, knowing that some will quit and the rest will stay because its too late to find another summer job. They take advantage of everyone, and when they get mad and quit, there's another naïve youngster waiting in line." My friend's sister was working there because she had been promised a chance at becoming a horse trainer,

something she loved. It became obvious that this was just a come on to get cheap office help, and she , one day, just walked out, not even telling anyone she was leaving.

Chapter 18 "The Great Kansas City Red Scare of 1962"

The summer of 1962 started off with great promise. (Its predecessor had been a huge fiscal blunder and I spent the year broke, in penance for my bad decisions.) I really needed to make some money and I landed a weekend gig with a mediocre quartet at "The Seven Keys Country Club". It wasn't much, but I was a working musician and still free to hunt a "day hang". Prosperity loomed. The first two weeks went fine, but then disaster struck. After the third week, in spite of having decent crowds, the paycheck bounced. The bandleader called a lawyer who told him to get in line, that every vendor in town was suing the place. (Years later, when I was a student at the Conservatory, The Seven Keys came up and a blues organist I knew told the story of when he had worked there, the old insufficient funds nemesis surfaced, yet again. By then, the place had burned half the bands in town, and the owner was a well know deadbeat. Figuring he would never see his money, the bandleader went in and distracted the club owner while the other guys loaded the club's pool table into the their van.)

I had graduated with a two year degree from Kansas City Junior College and was headed for what was then Kansas City University, a small midtown private college, that fall. My Mom and Dad would pay my tuition and buy my books, but the other expenses were on me. I had a very lovely and serious girlfriend, Margaret, (who would become my wife), a relationship I wanted to maintain, and going dutch wasn't in the lexicon. So the search was on.

Every day I would get up early, read the entire "help wanted" section of the want ads, write down anything that looked even vaguely promising, and burn up a bunch of gas driving all over town, filling out applications, none of which came to anything. I was so desperate that I went so far as to drive to Silby, Missouri, to pick strawberries. Bending over at the waist for four hours did me in. I cashed out and made precisely enough to pay for the gas down there and my hamburger and coke that I had for lunch. The only people who were making any money were

the migrant families with several children, all of whom who were able to pick much faster that I could. Finally, in desperation, I became the Ice Cream Man. Ice Cream was to be my destiny it seemed. When the company manager found out I was from Northeast, he all but turned cartwheels. He said they had a hard time keeping anyone on that route because there was a particularly aggressive independent who tried to intimidate the competition, and that applicants had been afraid of Northeast's reputation as the center of Kansas City organized crime. I assured him that I had lived there from 1948 till 1961, that I had many friends there and that I had never experienced any difficulty and didn't expect to. He said I was his man and handed me the keys to a white, WW II surplus Jeep with a canvas top and a freezer attached to the bed. So for a small percentage of the daily take, I became the man I had waited for, impatiently, my nickel in my hand, as a child. This was not what I had hoped for. By putting in 10 hours a day, including to and from and load-in time, I could make about $10 a day and days off weren't even discussed. I had no choice, I couldn't waste another summer, so I decided to make the best of the situation. I was back in my old neighborhood among friends, and was making some money. The Jeeps were open for the most part, there was no air conditioning, and if it rained and there was a cross wind, the canvas tops weren't much protection and you usually got soaked. So my days were spent yanking the handle that rang the bell, scanning the street for change bearing, hungry kids, peddling mostly Bomp Pops.

When fellow employees heard that I was a musician, everyone said that I should meet Will, an aspiring playwright working at the vending company, and they were anxious to make this happen. Will was a short, pudgy, moon-faced guy, with an unkempt shock of anarchist brown hair and round, steel rimmed, thick glasses. I never, ever, saw him in any clothing, but that which had Delight Vending Company embroidered on it. Will was supposed to be working as a mechanic, but if you wanted to talk to him, you had to find the Jeep he was sleeping under and wake him up. It seemed that he stayed up all night, writing, and then slept all day, under a Jeep, on the company clock. And, oh yes, Will was a devout devotee of one Leon Trotsky - as red as a ripe tomato. Now I've always been one to enjoy a colorful character and as an history major, I had taken United States Constitutional History 110. There was never anything in there making it illegal to be a commie. Will was as colorful as a Matamorous restaurant.

One rainy day, we struck up a conversation. He was quick to point out what a bunch of "bourgeois bastards" the company was. "Bourgeois bastards" was Will's favorite phrase. He assured me that they dealt from the bottom of the deck and that one had to watch their every move. For starters, you should always count everything. Cases of 12 were all too often 11 or even 10. (I checked and found out immediately, that he was right.) I asked him how he had gotten to be a mechanic. He chuckled and replied, "avarice". The company was so concerned about getting the money that he owed them, that they had given him a job as a grease monkey, (something for which he was ill qualified) so that they could make weekly deductions from his paycheck.

"How come you owe them money?" I inquired?

"Well I started out as a driver, but I had an accident, a collision with a parked car. They were really pissed and said that I would have to pay for the damage."

I asked him if the $1 a day they deducted for insurance wouldn't cover it?

"They said they weren't going to pay higher rates because of my carelessness. So then the capitalistic swine took me off the route and put me on the 'hot truck'."

I asked him what the "hot truck" was and he explained that on the really busy routes, the Jeeps wouldn't hold enough ice cream to service the entire route, so they would send a truck with more product to a daily rendezvous point. I asked him what had happened to that job.

"I had another accident. I ran the hot truck into the Jeep I was meeting. They were furious and said I would now have to pay for all three vehicles. They wanted to take my whole salary, but I told them I had to have enough for food and rent, so we agreed on a percentage."

"But you're still getting to them because you aren't doing anything."

"They're not only greedy bastards, they're stupid. They're too materialistic to just fire me and cut their losses."

There was no refuting Will's logic.

I seriously wondered how someone could manage to wreck three Jeeps and entertained the idea that it may have been deliberate. Later, a ride with Will quickly dispelled that notion. The consummate iconoclast, he never stopped for anything - red lights, stop signs or other cars. He would completely ignore all stop signs, but did give red lights some concession - he'd tap the brakes as he sailed through, an exercise he called a "St. Louis stop".

Will and I became good friends and everything he had told me about the company turned out to be true. The cases were frequently short, never long, and the amount of change I turned in everyday, never agreed with the company tally. A friend, E. T., had gotten a job there, worked three days, and had somehow lost $30. They didn't care if you quit, they'd just take the ice cream that you had bought, give the driver nothing for it, and sell it again. Will said it was a pissing contest between the drivers, many of whom were recent immigrants with poor English skills, and the company. Will's assessment became more obvious everyday. He was a very clever guy who was driven by righteous indignation that was common in most Socialists I knew. It was okay to steal from thieves. He told me how to order. The order forms you turned in every day to get your ice cream, listed the flavors on the right and the totals on the left. The orders were filled from the right side and charged from the left. So if I put, 2 dozen cherry, 2 dozen banana and 2 dozen orange bomb pops on the right, but put 5 dozen in the totals column, I would receive 6 but only pay for 5. This little ploy worked all summer and made up for the shortages, which the company would never admit to. As I've said, I have never been the guy who gets to make the rules, so if the rules are that there aren't any, then that's how I play.

Will and I began working on a play together, with him writing the script and me the musical score. Will's hero was Bertolt Brecht, the German Socialist playwright who wrote "*Die Dreigroshen Oper*", (The Threepenny Opera) and "City of Mahogany". (I owe Will a great debt of gratitude for introducing me to Brecht, for his early work was scored by Kurt Weill who became my absolute favorite theatre composer and I have spent a lifetime admiring his genius.)

One day a torrential rain storm made ice cream sales impossible. It was raining so hard that no one would come out and stand by the curb to buy a bomb pop. Will and I decided to go downtown for lunch. Will always operated on short bread so we settled on the Woolworth's lunch counter when Will saw a sign that said "All the spaghetti you can eat for 79 cents." We took a seat at the counter. Overcooked spaghetti with canned sauce is not among my favorites, so I ordered a club sandwich.

The food came and Will powered right through his spaghetti, which bore a striking resemblance to the industrial size cans of Chef Boy-ar-dee they had served at Northeast high school. He then summoned the waitress and informed her that he would like another plate. He hungrily scarfed it down as well as two more plates, totaling four.

When we received our bill, Will was alarmed to find that he had been charged for four plates of spaghetti, He exploded, yelling, "What is this bourgeois bullshit?" (Will detested the middle class). An indignant, surly manager quickly came over with a bellicose "What's the problem, bud?"

"The sign said all the spaghetti you can eat for $.79, yet you charge me for four plates."

"Well, one plate is all anyone can eat."

"Not me, I can eat four."

"Then you pay for four."

"No sir. The sign says all you can eat for $.79, so I pay $.79."

"You'll pay for four or I call our on-duty policeman."

"Go ahead on. Maybe you can explain to him how the sign says all you can eat but it doesn't mean it."

An elderly, uniformed, policeman sauntered over. Will liked the cops even less than he liked the middle class.

"What's the problem here boys?"

"This man refuses to pay his bill," the irate manager exclaimed, and stuck his index finger in Will's face for emphasis.

"That sign over there says all the spaghetti you can eat 79 cents." Will pointed at the sign. I'll be happy to pay 79 cents plus tax.

"Then what's the problem?" the policeman asked the manager.

"He ate four plates! You can only eat one for 79 cents."

"But it says all you can eat, it doesn't set any limit. The young man has a point."

The manager was trumped and didn't know what to say.

The policeman thought for a moment, then stated, "The sign says all you can eat. You can't charge him more than 79 cents."

We paid our bill and as we left the sullen manager shouted, "You two jerks never come in here again."

"Don't flatter yourself, asshole. That was the worst spaghetti I've ever eaten."

It was there that we got banned from the Woolworth's, but he didn't say whether it was the whole chain or just the one store. Finding the club sandwich stale and tasteless, this was no great loss to me.

The searing summer dragged by with me clanging my bell, 7 days a week, and Will sleeping under his Jeep *du jour*. The record breaking, stifling heat was good for my bank account, but not my spirit. I kept a personal stash of lime Bomp Pops for when the heat reached the saturation point. One particularly hot day, on Lawn Street, as I stopped for a sale, a huge, brown and white English Bulldog jumped up into the seat beside me, his mouth open and his jowls hanging, as he slobbered, hungrily, all over the seat. While non-violent, he made it obvious that he wasn't going anywhere till he got what he wanted. I pondered what do do with this canine extortionist, and then inspiration struck. I unwrapped an ice cream bar, then waved it in front of his nose, and threw it as far as I could. He leaped from the truck in hot pursuit, his ears flapping and stump of a tail wagging as he chased it down and consumed it in one gulp right there in the middle of the street. This re-occurred on the three following days. I asked the neighborhood kids, who thought the whole thing was hilarious, where the dog lived. I then turned off the motor, marched up to the door and knocked. An angelic looking elderly lady answered. I told her that she owned me thirty cents for the ice cream her dog had extorted, and if this was to continue, I would call the dog catcher. She laughed, gave me thirty cents, and promised to keep him in when she heard my bell. Then she bent down and gave him a big hug. It was obvious she really loved her big Churchill looking boy.

At the end of the summer, Will, E. T. and I decided, on a whim, to take a little road trip to Chicago before college resumed. I wanted to see the Chicago Art Instititue and the Shedd Aquarium, Will wanted to visit the headquarters of the Young Socialist Alliance and E. T. thought he knew where there was a whorehouse. So one night, after I finished my route, we all piled into my metallic blue '54 Ford sedan for the purpose of breakfasting in Chicago. One guy would drive while the other two slept. I took the first shift, drove till around midnight, then retired to the back seat for a little shut-eye. I woke up around four AM and peered up over the back seat. Will was driving like A. J. Foyt in the backstretch at Indy, weaving in and out of the big Kenworths and Macks, maintaining a speed of about 80 through traffic that was moving at about 60. Overcome by a sudden surge of preservation instinct, I tapped Will on the shoulder and told him I was ready to take over. We approached Chicago on northbound I-55 and began to wonder about how to get to downtown Chicago. We all knew the tune "Chicago" and the phrase "On State Street, that great Street…", so we decided we'd look for the State St. exit. That did the trick and we emerged on the loop in downtown Chicago around 10 AM. That was the biggest city with the tallest buildings any of us had seen, and we were impressed, We looked around for a place to park, a rarity in Chicago, and then we lucked out and stumbled on to The City of Chicago Parking Lot. We stashed the

Ford and began a serious search for some chow. We found a great little working class cafeteria, "Pincksley and Aylor's" the kind of place Will loved, and had brunch. E. T. hated it! Apparently, his diet consisted of cheeseburgers, French fries and cokes exclusively. "Don't they have a fucking McDonald's here?" he queried angrily.

We strolled, seeing downtown Chicago. Will had absolutely no respect for any authority of any kind, anywhere, ever! Positively none! I had heard the story from a friend about the time Will had been pulled over for speeding. As the policeman looked in the window, Will spoke, "I'll have a double cheeseburger, French fries and a cherry Coke." The man in blue was not amused as he filled out the citation, tore it from the pad and handed it to Will. I had learned that sucking up, contrition, an apology and a promise never to repeat the foul deed could sometimes get you out of a ticket. Not Will. I experienced some trepidation as we approached one of Chicago's finest, standing beside his three wheel Harley-Davidson Police motorcycle. Will thought their uniforms were funny with their checkerboard hats. He then walked over to the cop and said "I'd like a Fudgesicle, a cherry Popsicle and an Eskimo Pie, please." Amid chuckles from those passing by, the cop replied sharply, "You looking for trouble, smart-ass?" I'm sure Will had another zinger ready - he always did. But in this instance he showed a rare restraint, a wise decision in that this was the same crew that would be televised beating the crap out of everyone from Jerry Ruben to Dan Rather just six years later at the 1968 Democratic National Convention. We were young and didn't need much sleep. We pondered what to do first and I said the aquarium sounded good. E. T. said he wanted to get some "tail". Will's contribution was that the aquarium would probably be full of chicks - it was common knowledge that all women loved fish, so off we went. We also took in Grant Park and The Museum of Natural History. All of these spots were singularly lacking in "tail", E. T.'s favorite word. We looked for a cheap place to stay, found the YMCA Family Hotel, for $3.50 a night and checked in.

The following day the debate over what to do next resumed. Will pointed out that we had spent the previous day doing what I wanted and it was his turn. He wanted to visit the Young Socialist Alliance headquarters and since it was too far to walk and we only had one car, I should drive him around. E. T. thought we should address getting laid. Will and I decided to visit the YSA, since that was his reason for coming, and he had paid for one third of the gasoline. E. T. decided to free-lance the Loop to look for some "poontang".

I spent a boring day, in and out of offices, including "Fair Play For Cuba", every office redder than the previous one. Though I had several leftist friends, I had never been one. I was a staunch Kennedy Democrat. Giddy faced Will had found his promised land. "This is my kind of town", he happily proclaimed.

After a hard day in the political *unterlieben* of Chicago, we headed back to the Y. E. T. was drunk and declared that all Chicago women were "a bunch of tight-ass, stuck up fucking bitches." I assumed his quest for love had not been fulfilled. After dinner, Will declared that the Y was too rich for his blood and also too bourgeois. He had seen a sign for a dump called "The Acme Hotel - $1.50 a night". I emphasized that the place looked absolutely disreputable. Will said, none the less, that he was going to give it a go. He was sure, that as a writer, it would be an interesting experience. I walked over with him to register. It was the seediest place I've ever been in, with what appeared to be winos lounging around the tawdry, smoke-filled lobby.

Will strolled up to the registration desk and informed the clerk that he wanted a room. A hairy, unshaven man in a sleeveless cotton, ribbed undershirt, and a cigarette with an incredibly long ash hanging on his lip, just shook his head. Then he laughed and said, "Kid, this ain't no regular hotel this is a flop-house. You probably want the YMCA, a block over." Will grinned and replied, "I was over there and they told me, kid, you can't afford no regular hotel, you want a flop-house, and there's one a block over." "It's your funeral," the man replied as he extended the registration form. Will paid his buck and a half and signed "Jack Daniels".

E. T. had spent most of his money on beer and was in worse financial shape than Will. Trying to save money on parking, we had stashed my Ford in the alley behind the Y the previous night without mishap. E. T. said he would just sleep in the Ford. I gave him the spare key and felt some comfort in that E. T. would be standing guard and if my car were stolen or towed, E. T. would be there to call me and tell me where it was. Compared to my friends, I basked in luxury at the Y.

We finished off the trip with a visit to The Chicago Art Institute. There is a wonderful large painting there, a street scene in the rain, by Pizzarro, that is one of my favorites. After this, E. T. went into a rant on how he hadn't gotten to do anything he wanted to do and he was sorry he came. Will sarcastically snarled that everything E. T. wanted to do involved "nookie" and since neither he nor I had one, there was nothing we could do to help him. E. T. then said he wanted to go to the Rialto Burlesque Theater. Will and I decided that complying would be easier then listening to him complain all the way back.

The Rialto was as sleazy as the Acme Hotel. Cigarette smoke and the tang of cheap wine, Thunderbird and MD 20/20 filled the air.

Two clean-cut college kids and a scruffy radical looked strangely out of place among the derelicts and perverts that frequented that place. The Acme and the Rialto were like something out of Herman Hesse, one of Will's favorite writers. A series of over-the-hill, plump, saggy-breasted strippers strutted their stuff to canned music. As it was Sunday, it appeared that Chicago had some legal restrictions concerning nudity. E. T. was furious that not one had gotten past their g-strings or pasties. The last act was the headliner, and she was a spectacular, tall, well endowed raven-haired beauty. E. T. let out a whoop and yelled out, "Now that's a fucking woman." He leered at her every graceful move, issuing guttural utterances of approval. At the conclusion, the dancer appeared to be looking at the clock at the rear of the auditorium, and at the stroke of midnight, off came the pasties, revealing large bright pink nipples. E. T. about broke our eardrums. For a person totally obsessed with sex, E. T. appeared to get less action than anyone I knew.

As we headed for the car and the impending 500 mile all night drive, E. T. raved about the young dancer, extolling her assets in great detail, declaring she was Playboy material. E. T. was a self appointed expert who claimed to own a copy of every published Playboy issue. E. T. drove the first shift. At Will's request, I had brought along my guitar. Will knew every old W.P.A song from the thirties as well as most of the

Woody Guthrie and Pete Seeger repertoire,

two men who, at one point in their lives, had political views similar to Will's. Will would run through the melody so I could figure out the chord changes, then at triple goddamn forte, sing his heart out as I strummed - "Casey Jones, won a wooden medal, Casey Jones, doing mighty fine, Casey Jones, broke his god damn head off, that's what he got for scabbin' on the S.P. lines." But his favorite was "…there'll be pie in the sky when you die, that's a lie."

After frequent stops for E. T. to urinate from all the beer he had drunk, E. T and the car ran out of gas at the same time. It was his turn for the fill up, but he declared he was flat broke from the beer and the burlesque show, so I got stuck with his share. Will and I drove the rest of the way, and after I dropped E. T. and Will off, I went by Margaret's to tell her I was back and I loved her, then got home with fumes left in the tank and fifty cents in my pocket.

I got ready to start classes at KCU as a History & Government/Political Science major. I asked Will what his plans were now that the ice cream company had closed for the winter. He replied "Do nothing but write till my unemployment runs out." Will was a dichotomy - he detested the government, but had no qualms whatsoever about seeking its assistance any time he was in a bind, which was most of the time. Shortly after I had started classes, I got a late night call from Will.

"Ron, you've got to come get me. The bourgeois motherfuckers evicted me. They put all my stuff out on the curb. It's too cold to sleep in the park."

I fired up the Ford and picked him up. He didn't have much, just some dilapidated old junk which we loaded into the Ford's big trunk. I had twin beds in my room. I told him he could have the spare and we'd figure something out in the morning. Mom was very surprised that we had a guest and expressed her displeasure with the fact that the sheets on the bed Will had slept in were so dirty, that she'd probably have to throw them out. I told her Will didn't have a place to stay, so I was helping him out. Mom crossed her arms over her chest and stated emphatically, "Well he's not staying here." Whenever mom crossed her arms over her chest, you knew beyond a shadow of a doubt, that that was the end of the discussion. After breakfast, Will went with me to KCU and sat in the "Pouch", the student lounge, listening to the always playing juke box, arguing politics and playing chess. I broke the news to him that Mom had said he couldn't stay with us so we'd have to work out some other arrangement. I gave him some change and he made some calls to no avail. He finally said, for tonight, he'd just sleep in my car. Between

Will and E. T. I could have hung a "room for rent" sign on my sedan. For the next several days he slept in the Ford, then rode to school with me where I bought him some breakfast and he hung out in the Pouch. Finally, I told him that it was getting colder, winter loomed and he couldn't continue sleeping in my car.

"If I can get to Chicago, the Y.S.A. will help me out. There's no place for a Socialist here. This is one bourgeois damned town."

"How do you propose to accomplish that?"

"If you can let me have a couple of bucks and drop me off in eastern Independence on Highway 24, I'll hitchhike."

While doubting the sagacity if this plan, I desperately wanted to get him off my hands, so I agreed. I gave him my last five bucks and a roll of nickels I had, and drove him out to Highway 24, past Independence. With $7 dollars, a suitcase full of books, like David Schub's "Lenin" and "Listen Yankee" by C. Wright Mills, and a dirty pillow case full of worn clothes, all of which had "Delight Vending Co." embroidered on them, Will set out to change the world in a way he was convinced was for the better. He handed me a small package wrapped in a brown paper sack which he said I shouldn't open till I got home. It was a volume of "Nine Plays" by Bertolt Brecht, which had Kansas City Public Library stamped on the outside of the pages.

A few weeks after he had gone, literature starting appearing in my mailbox on a regular basis: "The Militant" the publication of the Y.S.A. and a "Fair Play for Cuba" chronicle, along with an assortment of similar newspapers. I received a letter from him saying things were going well and thanking me for my help. He also acknowledged having given several subscriptions to others, like me, whom had helped him. I had to make it a point to beat Mom out to the mailbox every day. If she had seen some of the propaganda Will had sent, she'd have been furious.

A year passed and Kansas City University became The University of Missouri At Kansas City and my cause became civil rights via my joining The Congress of Racial Equality. I had always been extremely liberal, but never anywhere near the area called "Red". The letters from Will stopped coming, but not the extremist publications. Then that fall President Kennedy was assassinated which broke all of our hearts. Shortly after that I ran into Will's old girlfriend, Maggie, between classes. She ran up to me and managed to look quizzical and embarrassed at the same time. She blurted out, "Ron, have men in black Chevrolets, black suits, hats and sunglasses been following you around?"

I replied, yes, and added that it was no doubt the result of the fact that, like Lee Harvey Oswald, Will had been an ardent member of the "Fair Play for Cuba". Maggie pondered for a moment and started chuckling. I soon joined her. It was, indeed, another gift from Will. Will had probably managed to get us on every subversive list that the FBI had by deluging us with Marxist literature. Maggie asked, "What are you going to do?"

"Just keep on being me and going to classes. They'll soon get bored with following a History and Government major around." They did.

My brief friendship with Will had long term ramifications. Thirty or so years later, I was hired to play a big band musical engagement at Whitman Air Force Base in some little town in rural Missouri. Whitman was a restricted base because of the B-2 Stealth bombers housed there and they had stringent security regulations. The band leader had to submit a list of players. I rode down in his van and when we reached the sentry gate, we were stopped. After a heated exchange, the bandleader had to assure them that he would assume personal responsibility for me and not let me out of his sight. I was, and am, a Democrat and the most radical thing I have done is support both Eugene McCarthy and George McGovern in presidential elections. At no time have I ever been a threat to, or advocated overthrow of my government, violently or peacefully. One of Will's favorite songs had been "The Ballad of Joe Hill" about a labor organizer who had been

beaten to death by management goons. The refrain is "Joe Hill is dead and gone, but his spirit lingers on". I sang loudly as the bandleader tried to smooze us in - "Joe McCarthy is dead
and gone, but his spirit lingers on."

I didn't see Will for 34 years. I married Margaret and she died young. Will married an African/American Chicagoan, who stabbed him, nearly killing him. I was at my friend, Marshall's, a prominent Kansas City Psychologist, for a barbecue. His brother, Tony, is my age and as we reminisced about the old days at KCU, Will's name came up. Tony said that Will was back in K.C. and gave me his phone number. I called Will and we agreed to meet at the Bryant's Barbecue on Paseo, which Will had always loved. I paid, of course! Give or take a few wrinkles and gray hairs, Will looked pretty much the same. While always prone to pudginess, he hadn't gained a lot of weight. He had, long ago, stopped writing but was still a very active Socialist who had run for Congress on the Socialist ticket in Wisconsin. He had lived in Milwaukee for many years. The fact that Socialism, as a world political entity, had been deemed a failed experiment and the Iron curtain had oxidized and fallen, had had very little impact on Will. He was as enthusiastic as ever and he believed what he believed, regardless of facts and was still very involved in radical politics. I was still composing and preoccupied with my music and production. I really enjoyed seeing Will again, even though we had nothing in common but some great memories of a very interesting summer.

Chapter 19 "John C. Dods III"

The mentor to a whole generation of Eastminster Presbyterian Church teenagers was John C. Dods III. The then young attorney was an imposing individual who looked more like a defensive end than the congenial, concerned, compassionate soul he was. We were always greeted personally (John always had a great memory for names and faces) with the bespectacled, twinkling eyes, and the big Dods grin. John had a way of making a person feel important, even when you weren't. Never one for religious dogma, he concerned himself with the moral and ethical issues of the day. His message was always clean and clear - first, think every situation through, from every possible angle and point of view, find the right thing and then do it! This was a refreshing approach. I had grown weary of memorized bible verses and religious litany. The truth was that the main reason, at 12 or 13, I still went to church was several really cute girls, (one of whom, a pretty auburn haired lass with freckles, I married in 1964). The hormones had driven me to the point of being a flaming heterosexual. I had lapsed into the pattern of ducking out on the long, boring archaic sermons, but I wouldn't have dreamed of missing one of John's weekly discussions. He was one of the most intelligent men and, perhaps, the clearest thinker that I have met in my entire life. John didn't offer pat answers, he posed questions for us to think through and find answers and solutions on our own. This was especially important to me. I had grown up with a father, of maybe slightly above average intelligence, who had dropped out of high school for financial reasons as a sophomore. His purpose for being seemed to be to tell my brother and me what to think on every issue, and dictate every decision for us right to the most insignificant details. He had already determined that I was going to be a lawyer and my brother a doctor. (You can imagine his disappointment when I became a jazz musician and my brother a gambler.) John appeared at precisely the right time. I well knew I did not accept the fifties' values of racism and the "My country, right or wrong" kind of patriotism personified by "Tail Gunner Joe" McCarthy that were being imposed upon me. John was the first person I had frequent contact with, who had been to college, except my school teachers, who kept their professional distance and weren't my friends. John was. He triggered a life long pattern for questioning what appeared to be obvious, not being afraid to swim upstream, and the realization that some issues are well worth taking a stand on, no matter what the consequences might be.

One of John's talks that I recall was about a famous legal dilemma that involved a lifeboat at sea with more people aboard than it could safely carry. A crewman picked out the weakest appearing individual, the one least likely to survive, and threw him overboard to drown. Did the sailor have the right, by virtue of his might, to impose his will for the greatest good for the greatest number at the expense of someone's life? This was a typical John C. Dods III Sunday School lesson.

Another that I well remember was John talking about trying to have lunch with an African/American law school friend. In 1957, while not Alabama or Mississippi, Kansas City was close - about as Jim Crow as they came. African/Americans were denied access to all restaurants, but Bretton's, movie theaters, swimming pools, hotels, motels, virtually all public facilities. They were also confined to a housing area bordered by Troost on the west, Brooklyn on the east, 9th Street on the north and 39th street on the south. If John wanted to have an inexpensive lunch with his friend, it would have to be standing up at the lunch counter at Woolworth's. That was the only inexpensive restaurant that would serve African/Americans, but they limited them to the standing only counter, they couldn't sit at one of the tables. John refused to stand up and eat a hot dog. Northeast, as I have noted, was an extremely segregated area with no contact with minorities, and we all grew up with blinders on. This was the first time that I had been confronted with the reality that minorities faced and it hit me like a "Sugar Ray' Robinson right cross. While at that time having neither the means, the independence, nor the confidence to address this issue, it really stuck in my brain as a future agenda.

A couple of years later, I was working, stocking the line with baked goods, at the Forum Cafeteria, which like every restaurant in KC, except the aforementioned Bretton's, did not serve people of color. A big sit-in occurred, which made national news - a group of well dressed African/Americans came in, joined the line, got trays, got salads, and when told to leave, refused to move, blocking the line and successfully shutting down the operation for the day. I remember admiring their courage and resolve. I became outraged at the expletive laced derision that the protestors were subjected to by Forum employees. The example I had had in front of me all my life, was that of my father - always shoot from the hip with an emotional, usually anger driven, poorly thought out reaction. I had decided, long ago that, while the instinct was there, I didn't want to be like my Dad. The person I knew who was the least like my Dad was John. My initial reaction was to take off my apron and hat, throw them on the floor, storm out in a tirade and join the sit-in, which would have surely cost me my much-needed job. Before I struck, I asked myself, "What would John do?" I quickly thought through the situation and realized that on one hand was a well organized, justified righteous indignation driven by purpose, with great tenacity. On the other hand was a management group, confused and disorganized, whose goal was that of most corporations, monetary gain. The fact was that there were no laws being broken here but a refusal to continue to accept the degradation of the way things had always been done. The demonstrators, as long as they were orderly, weren't breaking any laws. The police were called, but refused to intervene in what they perceived as a political and civil situation. There was nothing the Forum could do. Using the logic that I had learned from John, I had thought things through and quickly realized that the N.A.A.C.P would win this battle without any help from an outraged white youth. Using John's thought processes had saved me from a meaningless gesture that would have cost me much needed employment.

Corporate avarice trumped racism and The Forum was the second restaurant in Kansas City to break the chain. The Forum segued from a position of seeing the African/Americans as an inconvenience, to viewing them as a, heretofore, untapped source of new revenue. The Forum knew the game was ending and quickly agreed to serve Negroes if they came in in small numbers. The transition was smooth and without further incident. What I learned out of all this was that there would be many situations in life that are unjust and one could not address them all. What John had taught me is that it was pointless to fight if you could have no effect, or at least some small chance of winning. It would be better to bide your time and gather your resources and wait for a time when the odds were better. "It's better to burrow from within than throw stones from without" he used to say.

In 1963, at the age of 21, having matured and attained the moral fiber and the will to fight, I found myself at the corner of 27th and Prospect, as a member of the Congress of Racial Equality, passing out handbills, urging African/Americans to register and vote to support the Public Accommodations Bill which would make these segregationist practices illegal. There is not one doubt in my mind that this moment in time had its genesis in one of John's lectures. If my Dad had known I was there, he would have thrown me out of the house, but he was in New York, working for National Car Rental, setting up a leasing division. This was one of those incidents when the principles were well worth the fight, what ever consequences came as a result. We won that fight and Kansas City changed forever. The Public Accommodations Bill passed by a narrow margin and became law.

As if John wasn't already doing enough, he took over the Sunday evening Vesper services for teenagers. I think the Eastminster elders were intent on us not becoming juvenile delinquents. With the combination of John, and the aforementioned beauties, I was in. After the service it was our practice to all pile in a couple of cars and adjourn to Gino's Drive-In on Independence Avenue, close to the Sheffield bridge. John loved this place because it had been "The Griddle" where he had been a short order fry-cook as a high school student. I always ordered a "pizza burger", a hamburger with mozzarella cheese and marinara sauce, and a fountain cherry coke. Next, I would put a nickel in the juke box because it had recording of alto saxophonist, Earl Bostic, playing the haunting "Harlem Nocturne", which I loved. Then, the always practical John, would explain to me the false economy of juke boxes, that if I saved my nickels, I would soon accumulate 69 cents, at which point I could buy the record and hear it any time I want. My professional career had already had its humble beginning and I had a heavy dose of what is commonly referred to as "artistic temperament", a large portion of which is the need for instant gratification. I informed John that I already owned that record, but since I had an overwhelming need to hear that tune at that very instant, and the record was home, it wasn't doing me any good. Amused, John laughed and shook his head at what he viewed as my faulty logic.

The summer of 1961 my family moved away from Northeast and

in 1964 I became a college dropout for the first time to pursue a career in music. I ran into John from time to time and he seemed disappointed that I was no longer in college. I told him I was sowing my wild oats. I'm sure the not undeserved reputation musicians had as drunks and drug abusing derelicts was behind his concern.

"Don't sow them too widely, my friend," John said as he smiled and placed his hand on my shoulder.

Life raced by so rapidly and I evolved from a jazz wannabe to a was and John wasn't just any lawyer, but a really important attorney for a huge and very expensive international business law firm, Shook, Hardy and Bacon. Whenever I would have a minor legal concern I would call John and tell him to send me a bill. He was never too busy to help, and somehow, the bill never seemed to come.

In 1970 I had been on the road on and off for three years, and I'd had enough, as had the band I was working with - enough cheap hotels, enough 18 hour drives to the next gig, enough fast food. The road doesn't have the opportunities for secondary income that an ambitious individual like myself was always seeking, like studio work, or teaching. The band as a unit decided to give notice and return to Kansas City. I had my radar set on new opportunities and through a couple of friends I met promoting concerts, found a cheap and reliable source of phonograph records and we decided to open Bananafinch, a record store, and we three became partners. We opened on the northwest corner of 48th and Harrison in an old rounded store front, just a couple of blocks from U.M.K.C., which would provide a steady customer base, at least in theory. John gave his generous assistance with the legalities, leases, insurance, licenses and such. We put in some serious sweat equity, and while remodeling and preparing to open we found a closet door that was nailed shut. I called the landlady and asked her if the closet belonged to us or the adjacent apartments. She affirmed that it was ours. I asked Dennis, a big burly guy who was one of the partners, to grab a crowbar and pop the door open. He did and I heard a gasp and then a shriek of joy. I went over to see what all the fuss was about and there was Dennis drooling over a big wooden crate with maybe 25 lbs. of marijuana in it. Pot doesn't weigh much, so, believe me, we're talking a serious cache of reefer! Dennis, and Don, the other member of the triumvirate, were both devotees of the righteous weed and as such, immediately wanted to roll a humongous joint and fire it up. I had put in most of the money, and by that act, had become the senior partner. My training by John screamed out to think this thing through, which I did. I pointed out that, above all, I didn't want to get busted and that there were cops all over the neighborhood. But more importantly, this much dope was worth a lot of money and belonged to someone, and it was entirely possible that he could be some kind of badass with a ready means of retribution, who would take umbrage at us consuming his stash, maybe even to the point of kicking some serious ass, and that would be, of course, Dennis's, Don's and more important to me, mine. My partners pondered for a moment, torn between a huge supply of free reefer, and personal safety, and finally decided in favor of the latter. Then, not knowing what the next step was myself, I thought, who's the smartest person I know? The answer was easy, John C. Dods III. I called John and told him that there was an emergency and could he please come right over. He asked me what it was about and I told him I didn't think it prudent to discuss it over the phone. John did what he always did when he had a friend who was jammed up - he came, expeditiously, right over to the rescue. When we showed him the stash, a big smile lit up his face and he started laughing. He said we should call the police. I replied that, in view of the fact that Dennis, Don and I all had quite long hair, I was concerned that the cops just might bust us. They had been watching us with a suspicious eye since we'd started the remodeling. The other factor to consider was that the reefer was worth some serious dough and I didn't want some tough guy coming in with a couple of goons, asking me where it was. John said, "I see your problem." He thought for a few moments, then said, "Put the box back in the closet, nail it back up and from now on, the three of you have never heard anything about nor know nothing of it. If anyone asks you about it, police or otherwise, tell them to call me, your attorney." John was, in addition to his work at S. H. & B., a municipal judge in the city of Gladstone. He then asked, "As an officer of the court, I can legally be in possession of this, so can I have a little?" Dennis and Don started laughing and we gave him a small sample in a brown paper sack. We followed John's instructions to the letter. No one ever inquired about it, and to my knowledge, it was still there when they tore down the building about ten years later.

Other then occasionally running into John at social functions that I worked as a musician, I didn't see John again for about fifteen years. In the mid 80's, I became the musical contractor for "The Town Pavilion", an A. T. & T. owned mini shopping mall and office building at 11th St. and Main. We did a weekly lunchtime jazz concert called "Tuesday Tunes". The Town Pavillion was right across the street from John's office. As soon as he discovered I was playing there, he came for lunch every week and we got the chance to renew old memories over pizza.

In 1991, I was hired by my friend, trombonist Bill Drybread, to play an engagement that turned out to be the 40th reunion of the

Northeast High School, class of 1951, John's class. John literally glowed! He came up, got me off the bandstand at break time and took me around introduced me to his old friends, some of whom had younger siblings in my class. I was so pleased that he was proud of me.

In 2008, I ran into a local film maker, Joe Heyen, who was in the early stages of writing, directing and producing a documentary film about the Cowtown Ballroom, a popular Kansas City rock concert venue in the early 70s. As the former owner of Bananafinch, I was one of the people he was looking for. We had been a ticket outlet, thanks to my friendship with Stan Plesser, who had owned the Vanguard Coffehouse and the Cowtown. Joe was fascinated with the Bananafinch marijuana incident, and insisted on interviewing John and me for the film. Joe set a date at the Uptown Theater and I called the always accommodating John,who readily agreed to participate. I waited anxiously in the cold for my old friend to arrive. He showed up right on time. He looked great, much younger than his 72 years. We both had expanded around the middle just a bit. John had the wit, sharpness of memory, and curiosity of a much younger man. Toward the end of John's interview, Joe asked John if he realized that pot can be burned and smoked in small increments. John laughed and said he was a straight-laced lawyer who had never been to a rock concert. Joe then asked John outright if he had ever tried it. John, with a boyish gleam in his eye, said that the sack we had given him had sat on his refrigerator for several months. He said, one evening, he put some of it in a Kaywoode pipe, puffed, coughed and thought it was the worst stuff he had ever tasted, and he then threw the remainder into the trash. Joe shook his head in amazement.

Unfortunately, John's interview didn't make the film, but I was there, in all my glory for all of 15 seconds talking about Frank Zappa. I am so grateful to Joe for that day, because it was the last time I would see this wonderful man. At 74, John left this earth. Though, in a letter I sent him, I tired to tell him how important he had been in my formative years, I think maybe it was beyond words.

At John's funeral, the parking lot was full, and I waited in line for nearly an hour to pay my respects to John's family. As I left the visitation, the line was loner than ever, extending out of the building and on the sidewalk, nearly to the parking lot. It was obvious John had touched many more lives than just mine.

I like to think that I'm a good man and would have eventually gotten to my convictions on my own. Maybe so, but then maybe not. But one thing is certain, John sure sped up the process.

Good bye old friend, from one Viking to another. We'll never forget you.

Chapter 20 "Fool's Paradise"

I would like to preface this segment by saying Terry is doing great. He lives just a few miles from me and we get together for lunch a couple of times a month. He's 69 years old, having survived an exceptionally reckless youth, has a Master's degree in accounting, put his two daughters through college, has had a long, happy marriage with his second wife, Carla, and true to form, spent 13 years as a dealer at Harrah's Casino, before retiring this year.

I owe my brother a great debt. He raised so much hell, got into so much trouble, that Mom and Dad never noticed anything I did. I was always under the radar! I got away with everything.

Mom said when Grandpa died at 46, he left a lot of hell unraised, and Terry was carrying on for him, the life of every party. Terry got his penchant for gambling from my Dad. Dad always loved gadgets, and they would regularly turn up, a tape recorder, one time a wire recorder, or a new record player. Then they would disappear - a trip to the pawn shop after a losing week.

Mom always said that Terry would find the one kid in his class that was crazier than him, and that would be his new best friend. Mom got it right. Terry's best friend all through grade school was Tommy, the goofball.

Terry had an almost *a priori* affinity with numbers. He could always make them do anything he wanted. The other side of that coin was he couldn't diagram a sentence, even if a date with Sophia Loren had been the grand prize! Terry said. "I can read, I just don't retain anything." I was just the opposite. I always had a book in my hand, and had a way with words. I could sell anything, and always knew that at some point in my life, I would get around to becoming a writer. I'm also lucky to be able to count my paycheck. When we were kids, 9 or 10, as we listened to the baseball game on the old AM radio, Terry would figure the batter's current batting average, through his last at-bat, in his head, just for grins. Terry was a born gambler, and at an early age, always wanted to bet on everything. I stopped betting with Terry when I was 11 or 12 because I always lost. My Dad loved to play cards, and hated to lose, almost as much as Terry. At the age of 12, Terry could clean his clock in any card game, even when the old man cheated, which he was not above doing. Terry had an almost photographic memory for every card that had been played. Puberty and card counting came into his life at the same time.

When we hit high school, Terry's new crazy best friend was Bob, a half Italian opportunist who would do anything for a buck and could get them both into mob card games, via the Italian side of his family. He was also an All-City football star. Terry had become an exceptional snooker and bumper pool player. He had a great soft touch, and Bob was his muscle as Terry cleaned out foolhardy teenagers, full of braggadocio, more balls than brains. Terry was a born hustler, never flashy, he always played just well enough to win. He was a constant talker, taunting his opponents, trying to exasperate them, because, at that point, he owned them. He would look them in the eye, laugh, then confidently step to the table and stroke the ball softly for the winning shot. It would drift, slowly toward the hole, and just when you thought he hadn't put enough on the shot, it would hesitate, and plop into the pocket. Then Terry would hold out his hand for his cash. And if you didn't pony up, Bob would make you wish you had. And Terry wasn't just good at cards and pool, he was a generalist, not great at anything, but really good at pin-ball, the bar room version of shuffleboard, Terry could shoot with either hand, and every other bar and arcade game known to man. He also seemed to know, instinctively, who would win the big game on Sunday. (He could really piss you off!) He also had a bad temper and a big mouth, which he regularly used on cops. From the time I got my first car, I always kept fifty dollars in cash in case I needed to bail him out. One of the times Terry needed bailing out, I was at work and couldn't step up, so Dad got the call. I've told you about the literary societies - we were all Bentons and our arch-rivals were the Debaters. It seemed that a group of foul Debater , fiends had waylaid Terry's friend, Bill, who was the president of the Benton's, and, very much against his will, had relieved him of his trousers. Shortly after that, Terry and a few Bentons one night spotted Ray, the president of the Debaters, who had been one of the trouser theft incident perpetrators. Wanting to return the compliment, they chased him, but he was fast and made it to his car and sped off. Terry and his accomplices piled into his Chevy. The only car that would out run Terry's Chevy was George's 'custom '57. They soon caught up to Ray, who proceeded to drive toward the Shiel Police station. Now Terry viewed this as the quintessential chicken-shit act. If you got jammed up, you fought it out yourself, even if you got your ass kicked. You never, ever ran to the cops! They caught up to Ray as he pulled up in front of the station and, as Ray ran for the door, Terry stopped him with a flying tackle and went after Ray's Levis. Ray took a swing at Terry, at which point Terry decked him and really started pounding his ass. My Dad had to pick Terry up and you can imagine his fury when the Cop told Dad that as he pulled Terry off Ray, Terry had said, "Don't fuck with me man. Can't you see I'm busy." Terry was grounded for the rest of his youth after this incident.

Terry also started drinking in high school, as did all the dudes he ran with. For football games, they would buy a gallon of apple cider and a quart of Gallo White Port wine, which was just the right color, for 89 cents. Then they would pour half the cider out and top off the jug with the white port and walk right past the security personnel with the jug, sit up in the grandstand, cheer for Bob and the Vikings, and get a buzz on.

Terry was in one card game after another, always with a wad of cash in his wallet. And

he spent lavishly on good looking women, his third weakness. And being good looking, he always had several around. At one point, Terry had four girl friends named Judy. He said it simplified matters. He did fine in high school, acing every math course, algebra, geometry, trigonometry, calculus - his grasp of geometry was one of the reasons he was so good at pool. He did okay in everything else, and charmed his way through English, squeaking by. (He was lucky he had the affable Miss Davis who was really sweet. He didn't help his cause by referring to Shakespeare as "Shakyspeare"). The teachers knew he was bright from the standardized tests. In math, his scores were at the genius level, and they cut him some slack. By the time he graduated, feral Terry sported a Sal's Barber Shop special, "Flat top with fenders" haircut, had a spiffy '57 Chevy (that would run like a greyhound, but had crumby brakes, not a good combination, that's why it was in frequent wrecks), a movie camera and projector, guns, a slide camera, a fancy stereo, went to every sporting event and sat in box seats, bankrolled dates nearly every night, had a fat bank account and had left a string of broken hearts.

Terry also had some famous fights. Terry didn't have any particular pugilistic skills, and he wasn't that big, 5' 10" and 145 lbs, but he had a jaw cast in iron, was always inordinately strong and could summon an animal rage that gave him even more strength and made him impervious to pain. Once Terry got his hands on you, it was all over. It became a fact known both far and wide that no one in their right mind ever fucked with "Crazy Terry" Roberts. And the guys that were too big for Terry to handle, would have to deal with his even crazier friend Bob, who weighed in at about 225, all muscle!

My Dad, at our births, had decreed that we were both going to college. At graduation, I had three choices, I could go to college and major in what my Dad wanted, History and Government/Pre Law, move out and get a job like the one I already had at the Forum Cafeteria, not a viable option, or join the Army, something I would never, under any circumstances, ever have done. Hell, I was so opposed to the war in Viet Nam, I spent 10 years draft dodging, till the U.S. government decided that the trouble I would cause would far outweigh any possible benefit they may derive from my being in the military. (Being on every subversive list, thanks to my friend, “Red Will“, who had , inadvertently, been a great help in this regard, didn‘t hurt my cause.)

I decided to spend my Dad’s money on college as I bided my time, waiting for an
opportunity in the music business to pop up.

After Terry graduated, Dad declared it was time for Terry to follow me into the hallowed halls. His dream of Terry becoming a doctor had died when Terry threatened to beat the shit out of his high school biology teacher. Because of Terry’s prowess in math, Dad decided Terry would be an engineer. Now Terry was in no particular hurry to grow up - he was having too good a time as a teenager. Seeing our family struggles, he figured that adulthood just might not be all it was cracked up to be. He didn’t really want to start college, he just wanted to keep on doing what he was doing, being a good-time-Charlie, drinking, gambling, drag-racing his ‘57 at every stop light, chasing women and acting like a fool, which he had spent that summer doing, with great success I might add. When the time came, Mom rounded Terry up, put him in the car, drove him to Kansas City Junior College, where I was now a sophomore, and signed him up. Now if Mom had done her research, she would have found a college that wasn't just a half block from a pool hall! She failed Terry, miserably, in this regard. Terry had a whole new crop of suckers to prey on who didn't know about his expertise with a cue, and he quickly became the reigning "stick" and set up a "take on all comers" practice at said pool hall. Hell, they should have given him an office! He was raking in the dough. Now who should turn up at Junior College, but our old acquaintance Phil, the genius who had blown up the Cliff Drive Spring. By then he had alienated everyone we knew, with his mean-spirited pranks, bordering on sadism. Phil loved to gamble, he would have bet on a hop scotch game. However, he had a serious handicap for a gambler, he wasn't good at anything. He could play just well enough to make it

interesting for a very short time. He became a steady contributor to the Terry Roberts High Life fund. And the more he lost, the madder he got. Now Phil was bigger than Terry by a whole bunch, at 6' 1" and 200 hundred pounds. This tension was greatly exacerbated by the fact that if Terry didn't like you, he didn't just beat you. Constantly trash talking, he humiliated you in the process. And he had come to very much not like Phil. As I usually made it a practice to actually attend my classes, I didn't see the fight, but I ran into my friend Ralph, who could shoot a mean stick, in the parking lot. He had witnessed the event and said that it ended up with 145 lbs. of Terry, dragging 200 lbs. of a bloodied up Phil, around the gravel pool hall parking lot. Phil had found yet another thing he wasn't good at. I asked Terry about this, and he said, Phil had a good punch, but he was so slow, you could see it coming and stay out of the way. "Phil had no heart. You hit him four or five times and he was done." Phil, like most of the of the pool hall crowd, wasn't college material and was flunking out. After this humiliation, he dropped out of college and joined the army. This was not uncommon. It was peacetime and a good time to get mandatory military service out of the way. The total enrollment 2nd semester was appreciably lower than 1st semester.

In spite of cutting classes incessantly, Terry was still acing Calculus. The Calculus teacher one day walked west up 39th Street after class. He looked in the window and who should he see but Terry, crouched over the snooker table, cue in hand, cigarette in his mouth, lining up a tough shot. He was so angry that he walked back to the college office looked up our phone number and that evening called our house and got Dad. He told Dad that he didn't care how many A's Terry got on tests, if he continued to cut class, that he was going to flunk Terry. Dad's reaction to this was just short of an explosion at Los Alamos. Terry's grades were pathetic. The consummate optimist, Mom, with her rose colored glasses, always only saw the good in Terry and was blind to the many shortcomings of his youth. Upon seeing his grades, she and Dad yelled at Terry *ad nauseum.* They double teamed him - as soon as one's vocal chords would reach the point of incurring serious damage, the other would take over. Terry, who could muster tremendous remorse, contrition and sincerity when it suited his agenda, had his back to the wall and promised to do better. Then Mom, who was always in his corner, no matter what Terry did, went to the Dean of Students and made an impassioned mother's plea for them to give Terry another chance. Because of his standardized test scores, they agreed to give him one more semester on academic probation. If he didn't pull a C average, he was out. By mid-term, it was all over. Terry had just taken up where he had left off, king stud of the pool hall.

That was the first time Terry flunked out. He got a job in the mail room at a factory and kept right on indulging his vices.

Chapter 21 "Fool's Paradise Redux"

Terry's silver and white '57 Cherolet died a violent death. Terry was driving east on Independence avenue at a high rate of speed. Everywhere Terry went, he went in a big hurry. Someone turned left in front of him, and kaboom, Chevy gets totaled. Not even the great Uncle Clarence could fix it this time. Even though Terry's excessive speed was a factor, Terry dodged the ensuing law suit, (Jane, one of the passengers had a broken nose and a knee injury) by virtue of the fact that the other guy was failing to yield right of way and that trumped Terry's speeding.

Terry's new intermediate ride was a pristine, black 1952 Chevrolet that had been Mom's car. Mom had a new white Corvair so Terry bought the Chevy to use while he hunted for something with more cachet. Within a month, the little black Chevy looked like a New York taxicab - all four fenders had been crushed. Terry offered no explanation, but since the damage occurred in weekly increments, it was more than one incident. While being a math whiz, Terry seemed to be baffled by basic physics, the part about two objects being unable to occupy the same space at the same time.

I got up one morning to answer the door bell. It was an insurance man. Terry had applied for car insurance with a new company because the old one had canceled him after the last wreck. The guy asked to speak to Terry and I told him that Terry had caught a ride with a friend to work. He then asked me if that was Terry's car. I affirmed that it was. He went outside and walked around it, surveyed each damaged fender, one through four, wrote something down, shook his head in disbelief and started laughing out loud. Without saying a word, he got in his car and drove off and Terry never heard from him again.

This was Terry's introduction to the 40 hour a week work-a-day world and he was very unhappy. His friends were all in college, where someone of his intelligence should have been, and he was spending 8 hours a day sorting mail. He missed the action. Like most gamblers, with Terry, it wasn't the winning or the losing, it was the excitement of the risk. Terry was an adrenaline junkie. He found some card games to get into, but he missed his old running buddies.

Then, like a bolt out of the blue, fate stepped in and saw him through. Bob called. He was on a full ride football scholarship to Baker University, a small religious college in Baldwin, Kansas, about 40 miles southeast of Kansas City. There were several other former Viking football players there (Northeast had had a really good team). Bob urged Terry to enroll at Baker, enticing him by pointing out the Baker was an expensive private school and it was full of rich, naïve fraternity boys who thought they could play bridge. Bob needed a partner. Two smart operators like Terry and Bob could really clean up. That was all Terry needed and he began a campaign to convince Mom and Dad that he had matured and deserved a second chance at college. Mom and Dad, with some consternation, mulled this over. Dad had gotten a big salary increase when he went with National Car Rental and they figured what kind of trouble could Terry get into at a religious college. They seriously underestimated Terry's resolve to resume his life as a gambling, drinking, woman chasing hell raiser. His current status provided few opportunities to pursue these endeavors. Now if Mom and Dad had thought this through, they would have realized how easily Terry was tempted by bad influences and they would never have let him get anywhere near Bob. Terry won them over with his *faux* humility and sincerity. Terry couldn't wait to get back into the game.

The next semester rolled around and Terry was back in college, and this time he was 40 miles away where Mom and Dad couldn't even keep an eye on him. It didn't take long for disaster to rear its shaggy head. Terry's roommate was Jim, another former Viking on a football scholarship, an offensive lineman, who was every bit as looney as Terry and Bob. Terry was stunned to find that all students were required to attend "Chapel" and were assigned a seat so they could check attendance, and Chapel was at 7 AM, an anathema to a Saturday night party-animal like Terry. On Sunday, at that holy hour, Terry was usually comatose with a severe case of the morning after blues and wouldn't even be stirring or vertical for another four or five hours. Terry consulted his new roommate, Jim, on this dilemma, not a prudent move. Jim gave only two kinds of advice, really bad, and even worse. He told Terry that he should do what he did - pay another student to sit in his seat. When they took roll, Terry's seat would have an ass on it and that's all that they required. Terry implemented this plan, but the kid he hired was so dumb he sat in the wrong seat and Terry's seat remained assless. Terry was already in trouble the first week.

Terry did what he always did first, found female companionship. He quickly ferreted out the only wayward women at this small religious school. Then he implemented plan two and he and Bob became partners at a running bridge game that they set up. Bob had analyzed the situation exactly right. The school was full of well-heeled fraternity boys, full of swagger, but devoid of any semblance of street smarts, something Terry and Bob had in abundance, who thought they could play bridge. They were wrong and paid heavily for the lesson.

The next thing Terry did was find a bastion of culture, sophistication and higher learning, Marv, who owned Marv's Tavern.

The big game at Marv's was Ski-Ball, a game with rings of concentric circles, decreasing in size toward the center into which one tossed a small ball, with points accruing the closer you got to the center, the higher you scored. Now, as I've said, Terry had rare hand to eye coordination. (He had been a terrific slick-fielding short stop. If he'd had a throwing arm and could have hit, he might have had a career, but, alas, he didn't and couldn't.) He quickly mastered Ski-Ball and they played for beers. And as Terry had become the best player and was usually the big winner, he was shit-faced every night. Scratch the morning classes.

I went down to Baldwin to spend the weekend with Terry during Homecoming. I had

three friends, Bob, Jim and Don who were all starters for the football team. Terry had abandoned the dormitory in favor of a one room walk-up flat where he could pursue his quest for true love (ie the old in and out.) I knew, immediately he was in trouble. He looked like he was bleeding to death through the eyeballs. He rounded up some girls and we spent two nights of drinking, after which we poured Terry into my car. I was staying in the dorm with a friend of his so as not to interfere with the activity at Terry's Love Shack. The next day I went by about noon to see if he wanted to get lunch. He stumbled to the door in his jockey shorts, hungover, with lipstick smears all over his face, and looked quite miffed and slammed the door. Baker won the football game as Bob, a defensive tackle, made about a dozen tackles, Jim blocked terrifically as the African/American (One of very few at lily-white Baker) running back ran wild, and Don punted for great distance.

Back home, Mom asked me if Terry was taking care of business. Not wanting to rat Terry out, I mean what kind of low-life would rat out his only brother, I said he was. What I really meant was he was taking care of monkey business. Not too long after that, Mom got a call from a man identifying himself as the Dean of Students at Baker.

"Mrs. Roberts, your son Terry is not attending classes. All he is doing is drinking and gambling, and since no one in the dorm has any money left, he no longer has any reason to be here." It's a good thing my Dad was in New York. If he'd been home, there may have been a casualty.

When Terry got home, he complained that Bob had been guilty of every offense that he had, yet he had been expelled and Bob was still in school. I told Terry he had missed one of the basic tenants of life - the world makes exceptions for defensive tackles that make twelve tackles a game. Terry rejoined the work force with a job at a bank.

Six or seven years later, Terry was married, had two daughters,

Deborah and Michelle and a good job as an accountant at H & R Block Corporate Headquarters. Terry had always been ambitious, but up to now, he had been easily distracted. He decided to seek a degree in accounting at The University Of Missouri at Kansas City and made an appointment with a

counselor. The counselor looked at Terry's record, with two flunk outs, and was not encouraging, telling Terry that this was one of the worst academic records that he had ever seen.

Terry pointed out that he was married with a family, had a good job and had given up his prodigal ways and simply wanted a chance to prove himself. Because of Terry's high standardized tests scores in high school and his considerably above average IQ, the counselor acquiesced. He told Terry, emphatically, "This is absolutely your last chance. You should act like you haven't even been to college. It would take you twenty years just to get your grade point average up. I'm not going to make it easy on you. You get one semester, and if you don't pull a 3.5 point grade average, you're out. Is that clear?"

Terry stepped up and not only got the 3.5 grade point average, he got the degree, (with a little assist from his sister-in-law, English teacher Margaret, to get him through English) and another one. He has a Master's degree in Accounting. Terry finally grew up. He was having so much fun being a reckless kid, that it took him a bit longer than the rest of us.

Chapter 22 "Terry, Big Carl, The Mob and the River Quay War"

A fascination with gangsters has always been an American sociological phenomenon.

Cruel, cold-blooded killers like Jesse James, John Dillinger, Clyde Barrow and Bonnie Parker and, to some extent, even Al Capone, became romanticized into Robin Hood like folk heroes in spite of overwhelming evidence to the contrary. The disappointed, disenfranchised, marginalized lower class took some solace in seeing someone "stick it to the man."

In my old neighborhood, if you breathed and kept your eyes halfway open, you couldn't miss the evidence of organized crime at work - the pizza joint that never had any customers except a group of Sicilian types sitting at a rear table, who looked up suspiciously when you walked in, indignant about the interruption, or the bakery with the old guys at the back table behind the counter who gave you that "What-the fuck-do-you-want?" look when you came in to buy cannoli. It started in junior high school with junior league wise-guys selling parlay cards for sports bets on the playground. You could tell who the future players were by their entourage that always accompanied them. One guy I knew set up shop every day after school out of the trunk of his turquoise and white '55 Chevy, selling whatever had "fallen off a truck" that week - cigarettes, wallets, belts, ties… He was quite the pitchman: "Feel the leather in these Hickock belts". One day as I came out, I hear, "Hey Ronnie, come here, man, come on over. I got a great deal on Sunbeam electric knives. These won't last long." When I informed him that I had no need of that particular gadget, he replied, "Mother's day is coming".

One evening, as an ambitious 16 year old young musician with a bad rock 'n roll band, I played dog-house bass fiddle on the back of a flat-bed truck in the North End for a street dance. As we took a break, I observed a classmate, Petey, whom I hadn't seen for a while. I hoped he wouldn't notice me - no such luck!

"Hey *goomba*, how's your hammer hangin'? I didn't know youse was a musician."

"I haven't seen you in English class for a while, Petey."

"Those motherfuckers expelled me man! I was rolling jr. high kids for their lunch

money and some asshole snitched on me. Can you believe they threw my ass out over that bullshit?"

I feigned astonishment, knowing full well it wouldn't be healthy not to.

Halfway through the gig, the bandleader's son, who was a very naïve Raytown High football player who had no concept of the peril of his surroundings, cold-cocked a local character, “Little Sal”, who probably had it coming in spades. Suddenly, by some kind of telepathic process I suppose, Sicilian guys were all around the bandstand, flexing their muscles, popping their knuckles, looking quite menacing, waiting for us to get off the truck. It was like these guys came out of the sewers and garbage cans like racoons. At that point, I was glad I had run into Petey. I hoped that, when the melee started, he would intercede on my behalf, saving my life as this mob killed the rest of the band. An astute priest saw the situation and called the police who showed up just in time with a paddy wagon. But it wasn’t for the local toughs; they loaded us and our instruments in and escorted us out of there. The heat didn’t want any part of these guys any more than we did.

These hoodlums had some vicarious appeal to iconoclastic youth asserting their manhood, who enjoyed seeing someone thwart authority. They admired guys who could thumb their noses at John Law and get away with anything.

My brother and I had a very authoritarian father whom we both resented. As a result, we both had issues with authority figures. I was a strategist who would resort to clever means to circumvent and undermine those who would control my life, but Terry had only one play, a direct head-on frontal assault with all his guns blazing. Subtle was never in Terry's gestalt. In his youth, he believed with all his heart that every rule was made to be broken. A true gambler, 16, he had a half Italian friend who could get them into mob sanctioned card games. He was an exceptional card player and nothing was going to go awry at a sanctioned game. They were protected. The exhilaration of being able to get away with something had a definite allure for him. And he was always attracted to feral, explosive characters that fed his need for action, where he could bask in reflected glory. Terry won a lot, lost a little and everyone grew up except Terry. His half Italian running buddy ended up in the slammer and Terry married his ex-wife-to-be, a former nursing student he'd been dating/ Terry played it fairly straight for the most part. He still drank and gambled, but he's a really tough guy and no matter how hammered he got the night before, he could always get up, go to work, and function.

After getting his Masters, Terry kept changing jobs, getting salary increases with each change of team. Now for most of his youth, Terry had eagerly looked for trouble. But after he hit 30, he had matured and gotten past this and was chasing the great American dream of amassing enough go-to-hell money where he wouldn't have to take crap from anyone. This landed him in a position as Comptroller for a concrete company. When he first went to work for them, they were located out on Highway 71. They weren't mobbed up, but one of their employees was a certain "Big Carl" Spero, subject of many newspaper articles, at least one book, (The excellent Mobsters In Our Midst by former FBI agent, William Ouseley) and of interest to every federal, state and municipal investigative bureau in existence. This time trouble had found Terry in a bigger and more precarious manner than even he could have imagined, and for maybe the first time in his life, he was completely innocent. One of Terry's comptroller duties was to log the yards of concrete sold each week. He tallied this from weekly reports from the sales staff. His first contact with Big Carl was when Terry called him and really chewed him out for

never turning in his reports on time. Getting chewed out by my by brother is intense and usually involves more than token profanity. Carl came in, really steamed, looking for Terry. Carl's boss

told him that Terry was just doing his job. Carl stomped into Terry's office and told Terry that since Terry didn't know who he was, he was giving him a one time benefit of a doubt. "I like you. You've got balls. But if you ever talk to me like that again, man, you're gonna have a big problem. Ask around and see what that means." Terry did and Carl's point was well taken. Then the company moved to the North End and

Terry moved with it.

The River Quay began when Marion Trozzolo, who was a wealthy entrepreneur and former college professor, had a vision. He wanted to gentrify the area, turn the tawdry, mostly vacant North End into a riverside mini-mall of boutiques, cafes, and night clubs, a family entertainment center like those he had seen in Europe. He bought up much of the real estate and established an owner's organization that featured a covenant that prohibited everything but clean entertainment - no strip joints or go-go girls! It worked exceedingly well for a while. The restaurants and night clubs were packed and shoppers lined the streets every weekend as they perused the shops and boutiques. A spectacular success at first, it became the weekend destination point. But the old line Mafiosi owned some of the property. Urban renewal and a big hotel project had cleaned out West 12th St. where the Comasano brothers had had their action, a bunch of strip joints that they had used as the base for their prostitution operation. They were looking for new turf. One of the main River Quay players was Fred Bonadonna, who owned a restaurant/night club called "Poor Freddie's". Bonadonna was the president of the Owner's Association and was vehemently opposed to strip-joints, which ran him afoul of the Comasanos. For his troubles, he was rewarded with his father's dead body in the trunk of his car. Then, pn property the mob owned, an X rated pornographic movie house, the Old Chelsea opened. Bodies started turning up regularly and places blew up. Poor Trozzolo, who was a good man, completely legitimate in every way, watched his dream and heavy investment evaporate amidst a hail of bullets. Avarice, power lust and stupidity was ruining it for everyone. And when the money stopped pouring in, buildings that were over insured started blowing up regularly in gas explosions. One guy was so dumb he got busted for attempted arson. He had cut the gas line in three places and it still didn't blow up.

Carl Spero, who had an old grudge to settle over the death of his older brother Vince, made a power play and enthusiastically cast himself right in the middle of all this, which was incredibly obtuse because he never had the openers to be a made-man - he wasn't all Sicilian. He was half Greek.

Spero had been a guest of the federal government at the big gray motel in Leavenworth, Kansas for beating a jewel courier nearly to death in an attempted robbery. The rumor was that strings had been pulled to get him out of the joint early to do a "job" for underworld kingpins. His cover was a sales job at the supply company where Terry was the recently hired comptroller. Like many psychopaths, Spero had a very charming side and was very funny in a goofy sort of way. Terry is extremely gregarious and has always made friends easily. He quickly adjusted to his new surroundings in the North End, and found a place, Cascone's Grill, where he loved to have breakfast, and he became a regular at the bar at Jennie's Ristorante which had an entertaining bartender, Hugo, whom he liked. He loves having people around. He also has had a long time fascination with loose cannon characters who generate excitement. He and Carl clicked. Terry viewed Spero as a funny cliché, a harmless, Runyonesque gangster. (While Terry knew Carl was involved in organized crime, he had no idea that Carl's resume included the vocation of "hit man".) Big Carl liked to gamble, but was losing money on sport's wagers, something Terry excelled at. For all of Terry's life he had the facility to make maybe 6 bets and 4 or 5 of them would come up winners. He knew the mathematics of gambling, how to spread out his action and which teams were covering the spreads. Terry helped Carl with sports wagers.

Terry began to get some idea of Carl's juice while he was having lunch one day in a dubious North End barbecue joint. Carl had given Terry his business card, telling Terry that if anyone in the North End gave him any shit, to show them his card. After Terry finished his brisket sandwich and fries, a minor guido started leaning on Terry to join the card game up- stairs. Terry told him no thanks, that he had to get back to work.

The guy took Terry by the arm and became quite insistent. Terry got out his wallet and showed the punk Carl's card. The guy looked really shocked and began to apolgize profusely, telling Terry that lunch was on him. Terry said no, that he'd pay for his lunch and go his way and that would be the end of it.

The next adventure involving Carl was at the annual Golden Gloves amateur boxing matches. Dad, as a youth, had fought in the Gloves and he loved to go every year so Terry always took him. Carl had been a prominent Golden Gloves heavyweight with a string of flashy knockouts so he also always attended. After the fights, Terry and Dad returned to the car in the nearly deserted Municipal Auditorium Garage, only to find three surly looking young hoods with obvious bad intentions, waiting. Terry was wondering what to do, trying to decide whether he should fight or flee when he heard Carl's voice from a distance. "Terry, are you all right?" Terry replied, "No Carl, I'm not!" Carl pulled a large caliber automatic pistol, with a highly illegal silencer attached, out of his belt and fired two rounds into the ceiling of the garage. Terry said it went "pop pop", you could barely hear it. Seeing chunks of concrete shrapnel as they echoed and splattered to the floor, the punks got the message and quickly scattered. Dad inquired, "Who the hell was that?"

Terry replied, "Carl Spero."

"I think maybe I'd stay away from him."

"In case you didn't notice, he just saved your ass!"

Guys were getting whacked. A high up made-man got clipped at his home, a definite breach of La Cosa Nostra protocol of the highest order. Two of Carl's friends, who were suspected of having committed this dastardly deed, turned the key to start their car one day on Truman Rd. They found pieces of them six blocks away after the explosion, a message hit if there ever was one. One was an acquaintance of Terry's and he quickly got the picture that Big Carl was about as harmless as a cobra and being his friend wasn't the safest thing to be. According to the Kansas City Star, Carl was at loggerheads with the Comasano brothers, the pair that were pushing the action for strip joints and go-go girls in the River Quay, because he believed they had been instrumental in the death of his brother. The Comasano brothers were two really bad men.

One day Terry was at work and in walked a pair of black suits who flashed identification as FBI agents.

"We want all of Carl Spero's records," demanded the black suits.

Terry did some fast thinking. He well knew the score. He'd been educated in it for 18 years as a Northeast resident. You never, ever, snitch on anybody for even the slightest offense - to do so could make your next address the city morgue with a tag attached to your big toe.

Terry never liked cops of any kind anyway and was born with an intensely truculent mind set.

"You guys got any kind of paper, a search warrant for instance?"

"No, but we can sure as hell get one," assured one of the black suits.

"What do you mean coming in here with that bullshit? I would recommend that you two motherfuckers get your asses out of here and don't come back till you have one and stop wasting my goddam time!"

The black suits glowered at Terry and hustled out the door.

In the short time he had before he knew the agents would return, Terry did some fast thinking and got the name of Carl's mouthpiece and had him pick up all Carl's records. Terry understood the deal. The FBI wouldn't kill him, but Big Carl might. When the black suits returned, Terry told them that all the records were with Carl's attorney and they could take up the matter with him. After that incident, Carl couldn't do enough for Terry. He treated Terry like his best friend and asked him if he could help him in any way, did anyone owe Terry any money? Then one day Carl asked Terry if he ever went up to Omaha to play the horses. Terry replied he was going that very weekend. Carl asked Terry how much he was going to bet. Terry replied maybe a couple of hundred. (Since Terry became a family man, he didn't lay down the big roll like he had in the past, but he did still like to "dip his beak".)

Carl said, "Man, I really appreciate you stepping up for me. You're a stand-up guy! I'm gonna do you a big favor." He then gave Terry a list of horse numbers for each race and told him to, every time he won, let the whole wad ride on the next race, and not to deviate from the scheme in any way. Terry and his ex-wife-to-be made the drive up to Omaha and, carefully following Carl's instructions, Terry started placing his bets in the prescribed manner. $200 quickly became $3,500. At this point Terry knew for absolute sure that the fix was in, information that a peckerwood is seldom privy to. Terry got up to go place the next bet and his ex-wife-to-be went completely bananas. She screamed, "Terry, if you bet one more dime, I'm filing for a divorce!"

Terry replied, "We're up $3,500! I don't see what you're bitching about?" The ex-wife-to-be was not moved by Terry's logic and started walking toward the car, so Terry gave in. At a recent lunch when Terry was telling me about this episode, Terry said, "She went completely berserk on my ass so we split. I should have left that mackerel snapping bitch right then and there. If I'd have stayed, I'd have won $70,000!"

Terry, who sometimes thinks he's invincible, continued to see Carl socially because he figured to not do so was lunacy. The River Quay war heated up and the place became as deserted as a graveyard. Dodging bullets is not a pleasing prospect. I was working in the area at that time at a restaurant that was owned by a couple of non-connected Italian brothers, doing a jazz duo with a fine singer/pianist, Carol Comer. The building had been their Mom & Dad's long closed family neighborhood grocery store. The brothers had inherited the structure, remodeled and opened a really nice Italian eatery. In one week's time it went from a packed house to completely empty chairs. The mobsters had ruined the action for everyone, including themselves!

One morning I got up, walked out and picked up the newspaper, walked back in and sat down at the table to a cup of Suisse Mocha and a bowl of Wheaties. I opened the paper and

nearly fell over backwards in shock. I knew of my brother's relationship with Carl. The front page story read that Carl had been drinking with his brother at a place he hung out at, the Virginia Tavern on Admiral Boulevard. For a marked man, this was not a sapient move. The first rule of mob related survival is you don't establish predictable behavioral patterns. While Carl sat and drank with his brother, three masked gunmen snuck in and opened fire at point black range with sawed-off shotguns. Carl's brother was hit and died instantly. Carl took a blast in the back, fell in a pool of blood and was left for dead as the hit-men made a hurried getaway. The assasins had no idea just how tough Carl was. When the police arrived, they found Carl's brother dead, and a trail of Carl's blood which they followed out of the tavern, into the parking lot. They found Carl passed out by his Cadillac with the driver's side door open. Under the front seat, they found Carl's piece, a 12 gauge with the double barrel shortened by a foot. Carl had taken a blast in the back that had severed his spinal cord, and, while gravely wounded, with his legs rendered useless, had managed to pull himself with his arms, out of the bar and across the parking lot before he became unconscious from blood loss. He was arming himself to return to the fight!

Extremely concerned, I immediately called Terry. He was stunned beyond words and considerably apprehensive about his immediate well being. The papers were full of accounts and analysis of these events. Carl's whereabouts were a mystery. Then one day about a month later, Terry was at work. The phone rang and it was Big Carl. He told Terry that he was at the Burns Hospital in Denver, a place that specialized in nerve damage. This was information that placed Terry in grave peril. Carl declared, confidently, with his old bluster, "Terry, they really fucked up. I still have a trigger finger and when I get back to

Kansas City, there isn't going to be any more Mafia problem."

Terry told me about this and I urged him to keep his mouth shut - that kind of

information could be lethal.

As if Terry didn't have enough problems, he then, out of the blue, got a summons from the Federal Grand Jury. He consulted an attorney and was told he had no say in the matter. Failure to appear would result in a contempt citation and issuance of a bench warrant for his immediate arrest. So Terry put on his best suit and very nervously drove to the Ninth District Federal Court. He went in and sat, tensely, till he was called, then took his seat in the witness chair. The judge looked at Terry grimly and asked, "Mr. Roberts, what do you know about Carl Spero?"

"Your honor, I don't know any such person as Carl Spero," Terry lied.

"Come now Mr. Roberts, do you really think we're that stupid?"

Terry's defense when he's frightened is always rage, and he fired back. "Evidently you're not as smart as you look", was his ireful reply. "I have two young daughters. I'm an accountant and I'm just trying to make a living. You can do anything to me you want, put me in jail, whatever - I'm never going to know any Carl Spero. You get the picture?" Like I said, Terry knew the score.

The judge was as smart as he looked, and seeing Terry's cogent point, kicked him loose.

Big Carl rode back into the Kansas City panorama in a wheel chair, a paraplegic. He had a hand controlled white Cadillac parade float back in the days when Cadillac's were about a half block long. As if this wasn't ostentatious enough, it had a personalized license plate, SPERO.

If he was intimidated, he certainly didn't show it. Terry had always said that Carl was absolutely fearless (apparently to the point of absurdity). The Kansas City Star did a story on Carl's return and the reporter was amazed at how conspicuous Carl was making himself. They theorized that he had a death wish and was deliberately making himself a target. I called Terry and told him about the article and to stay away from Carl and, under no circumstances, should he get into Carl's convertible. Starter bombs seemed to be the standard means of retaliation for Carl's adversaries and a car bomb could not distinguish between the intended victim and innocent bystanders. Terry assured me that he had gotten the message and that he wasn't hanging out in the River Quay at all. He was going to work and coming straight home. This is one of the rare times in Terry's life when he was truly frightened.

Carl opened up a Downtown used car lot and went into business. There was a small "shack" for an office. One day, not too long after his return, the shack blew sky high, scattering pieces of Carl over several blocks. The Camasanos weren't savvy enough to understand electronic surveillance and wire taps. The FBI had made their phone months ago and had a tape of Willie Comasano saying, "I don't care if he's fucking crippled, I want the motherfucker dead! Do you understand me? Dead!" After Carl's death, a series of high profile arrests ensued, including both of the Camasanos and their henchmen, and this time the feds got convictions. Old Italian men died in the federal penitentiary. Carl's threat had been accurate, though not in the manner he had boasted about. The Las Vegas skimming scam brilliantly portrayed in the Scorcese movie, "Casino", had made redundant the top echelon of the old line Kansas City mob. Spero's death had resulted in the next tier going to the big house. Kansas City still had something of a Mafia problem, but a much diminished version.

Shortly after that, Big Carl's only remaining living brother blew himself up in a failed attempt to construct a car bomb. That cleaned the slate. All five Spero brothers had died Mafia related violent deaths.

Terry continued to gamble, but instead of local action, he opted for the kitch of Las Vegas. He did pretty well till they went to the six deck boot. Years later Terry and I were discussing this episode with regard to his relationship with Carl, over pasta at our new favorite Italian hangout, Avelutto's Italian Delight, in Mission, Kansas. "Big Carl's wife died. She choked on her food," Terry stated. Carl's wife was described as a beautiful, voluptuous former stripper by Terry and publications. Famed hit-man Richard "The Iceman" Kuklinski", was interviewed in Phillip Carlo's book Iceman. Kuklinski's escapades seldom involved anything but homicide in its infinite variations. Kuklinski stated that Cyanide poisoning, something he had much expertise in, is extremely difficult for pathologists to detect. One has to be looking specifically for it. Cyanide poisoning is usually diagnosed as asphyxiation from esophageal blockage by food. When I informed Terry of this, you could all but see the light bulb blink on over his head. "That makes sense," was his reply. "They killed her too."

The years raced by and Terry and I both retired. Terry's ex-wife-to-be became his ex-wife and he married Carla, an act he regarded as a definite spousal upgrade. I read William Ouseley's remarkable book, Mobsters In Our Midst then passed it on to my brother. Then one day, between bites of spaghetti with peppers and Italian sausage, Terry commented on how much he'd liked the book. I asked him how many of those guys he had known.

"About half of them. A couple of them were at my 50th high school reunion. You know, I'm really lucky to be alive."

But then, he always was "Lucky Terry" Roberts!*

* Terry continued to gamble in his later life, but he found a surefire way to beat house odds. He changed teams. His work for the last 15 years prior to his retiring in 2010, was as a Black-jack dealer at Harrah's Casino in Kansas City.

Chapter 23 "Margaret Sue Laughlin Roberts"

On 12-15-12 it will be 34 years since Margaret ceased to be. In some ways it seems like another lifetime, and in other ways it seems like only yesterday and is still an open wound. I have thought about her every day of every one of those 34 years. She is part of me and will always be so. If you accept the premise that you're not dead till the last person who knew you dies, then she is still very much alive in me and the thousands of students she taught.

I met her when her family moved to Kansas City in mid school year from Mack's Creek, Missouri, in the Ozarks in 1953. We were 10 years old and in the 5th grade. She was a cute auburn haired, freckle faced bundle of sunlight, always smiling and energetic. She seemed rather sophisticated. She spoke very precisely with no trace of a country, "Hill-Billy" accent the kids who came in from the country invariably had. It was obvious she was bright and intellectually eager. Both of us were aggressive alpha type personalities and academic competitors, and we clashed at first. She was the "new girl," but it didn't take her long to establish a group of devoted friends. I had been the "teacher's pet' because, unlike many of my male classmates, I never got into any trouble and Miss Whitaker, our teacher, placed a great emphasis on music, something I was really good at. The always competitive Margaret came gunning for me! She was really good in English, but had no talent for music, which was everything to Miss Whitaker. Even then I thought she over emphasized it, embarrassing tone deaf kids by making them sing solos. (I thought it was ludicrous then and still do.) On the play ground, I found Margaret amusing - while not the least bit athletic, she seemed to really enjoy the sports and always gave it her all. That was one of her qualities, she really knew how to enjoy herself. She also revealed her half Irish temper, blowing up to anyone with the temerity to call her "Maggie". She was never, or ever would be, Maggie.

The next year we were in the 6th grade together in a "split room", a divided 6th grade 7th grade class, something they did with the bright kids from the lower grade. The competition between us really heated up. She thought I was cocky and needed to be taken down a notch. She was probably right. By that time, I knew I was bright and confident in the fact. I never believed in hiding my light. Margaret was every bit as confident as I was and intellectually, while having different talents, we were dead even I think. Margaret was more competitive academically than I ever was. If I really want something, I'm as aggressive as they come, but academe just never mattered that much to me. The regimentation was a factor I'm sure, and I have never functioned well in groups. Margaret did.

In the 6th grade, I had seen the movie “The Great Dorseys”, and had made up my mind, for good, what my life would be, that of a musician. Margaret was grade conscious and wanted to be at the top of the class. I didn’t care. I knew academe, for me, wasn’t part of the lexicon and I made little effort to establish academic credentials, but managed to get good grades anyway. Though I knew I needed to be educated, and school was always easy for me, I never much liked it and never had any interest in jumping through hoops for teachers to make a grade. I detested the kids who gathered around the teacher’s desk after class, sucking up, telling teachers what they wanted to hear. Margaret loved school. She reveled in academe. It was her natural habitat. For the first time in my scholastic life, someone scored higher than I did in reading. Mrs. Cribbis administered a standardized reading test. I scored at a 12th grade level. Margaret was already in college! She could read faster with greater retention than anyone I’ve ever met. We slugged it out for the rest of the year.

In the 7th grade, we had a choice, we could advance to Northeast Jr. High, or stay at Scarritt Elementary. My mother made my decision for me. She declared that I would stay at Scarritt so Terry and I could advance to N. E. Jr. together. It was the worst thing that could have happened to me. All the bright kids, except my friend Carol, went on to N. E. Jr. and the slower kids stayed at Scarritt. Margaret was among the former so I didn't see her for a year. Mrs. Cribbis was at a loss at what to do with me. She knew I was talented, but I was stuck in a group of slow learners, as was Carol. I was miserable, and did what I always did when I was unhappy, retreated to my fantasy world, writing music in my head, day dreaming of the days I would be a touring musician, seeing the country, and reading voraciously. I had discovered Jules Verne and H. G. Wells.

I continued to see Margaret in Sunday school and already knew that at some point, she'd be the girl for me. I understood that this was not my time, but merely the warm-up for what lie ahead, waiting around the bend.

In 1955, Terry and I matriculated to Northeast Jr. I saw Margaret at school again. She was taller and very slender. As we had no classes together, we were no longer competitors. Because of academic indifference on my part, I had been branded an underachiever in spite of making good grades, and was not part of the accelerated classes. Margaret was. I had to keep my career plans to myself. My Dad was determined he had sired a lawyer, and wanted no part of a drunken bum, woman chasing musician in the family (something I never in my entire career, ever was). So I took a lot of history and speech classes toward a career in jurisprudence.

My freshman year, I made a life changing decision. I gave up the violin and became a bassist. A year and a half later, I got into a rock 'n roll band, and I became even more certain of the arc my life would take. I didn't see Margaret much except at Sunday School, where there was little opportunity for social discourse.

My sophomore year, a friend of mine started dating her, which concerned me and spurred me into action. For my 16th birthday, I took Margaret to see Cinerama at the Midland theater. We rode the bus, something she was used to. Her father had abandoned the family and was giving no support, and her mother didn't drive. Margaret had softened since our elementary school days. I think the scandal of her father running off with a 15 year old girl who was pregnant took some of the starch out of her. I was taken aback at how poor her family was. They

lived in a tiny house with Margaret and her sister, Judy, sharing a bedroom . Her mother had a small bed and slept in an alcove. We had been that poor early on, but that was behind us now. Margaret and I dated for a few months and were having a good time, seeing movies which we both loved and talking about literature. I was amazed at how much she had read. She introduced me to the poem, "Invictus" by William Ernest Henley, which became a life long inspiration. My time with her was the best time. She really enjoyed art, but hadn't had many opportunities to pursue it. Then my Dad did what he always did, anytime I was happy. He fouled it up. He told me I was too young to single out one girl, that I should be playing the field, and that I couldn't see Margaret any more. I didn't want to date other girls. Margaret was the one. So I retreated into my fantasy world, living in my dreams and books. That's what creative kids do when things aren't going well. We have an escape valve, a parallel life in the imagination. Then my Dad would yell at me for walking around like I was in a daze. He was determined to screw up my life and I was just as determined that he wouldn't and that I would never become an overbearing, over-confident tyrant like he was. I got my own car and became a regular at the "beatnik" coffee houses where the aspiring artists gathered. That became my element.

I continued to see Margaret at Sunday School. She was the reason I still went.

After graduation I worked at the Forum Cafeteria and dated another freckle faced red-head named Jeanne, till my Dad gave me the old playing the field talk. Then at the end of the summer I met Rita. I was up at Jim's house. His sister, Sandra, had brought Rita, a cute fellow nursing student, to go on a double date with two guys Sandra had met. Rita took one look at the homely, overweight pair as they walked up to the house and told Sandra that she wasn't going out with either one of those guys, that she'd rather go out with me. I told her that was fine by me and we went out the back door as the two guys knocked at the front. We went to the Lawrence Gallery coffee house where all the hipsters hung out and ate Andre's pastries and sipped espresso as we listened to folk music. Sandra wouldn't speak to me for over a year because of this episode.

The fall of 1960 I began my college years at Kansas City Junior College. I was very
happy to see Margaret there. I wasn't surprised. I knew we were supposed to eventually be
together so she would have had to be there. The Northeast kids made it a practice to lunch together, so I saw Margaret frequently. She was in her milieu, luminous with excitement about the opportunity to learn. She was born to go to college. I think she would have been happy to have been a college student her entire life. It was obvious that she was dating someone so I continued dating Rita for a while, knowing in my heart that my time would soon be at hand.

Then Margaret really shocked everyone at Eastminster Presbyterian. She brought an African/American friend she had met in college, Hortense, to the service, probably the first black person who'd ever been in that church. Rev. Crockett, a good man in every way, smiled and told Hortense, sincerely, how welcome she was. Most of the congregation, however, did not share his magnanimity. Margaret did things like that. She was quiet and non-confrontational for the most part, then after she'd lulled you into a false security, she'd sneak in a haymaker. I was very impressed with her social conscience and fortitude.

Then the confluence I'd been waiting for occurred and it was goodby Rita. Margaret and I started dating for real second semester, and there was nothing my Dad, or anyone else was going to do that would change that fact. I had rounded that bend and my life was no longer in a holding pattern. I was dating the girl I'd been waiting for and I was playing bass with the Addie Weber Sextet, my natural habitat. Margaret indicated that she wanted to be able to help her mother more, and if she could learn to drive, her Dad, whom she had reconciled with in spite of his randy behavior, would help her get a car and she could drive her mother to the grocery store and in bad weather, to the bus stop for the ride to Montgomery Ward's where she worked. I was happy to help

Margaret in any way I could. Daily driving lessons in my '54 Chevy began up on Gladstone Blvd. where there wasn't much traffic. Life was coming my way at last and for the first time in a long time, I was truly happy.

We continued going out every Friday and Saturday. Because of a dearth of family funds, Margaret hadn't been to restaurants very much. I was driving a delivery truck for a cleaners part time and working some weekend gigs with a borrowed bass, so I had some disposable income which I invested in some fine dining which she really enjoyed. We had a Psychology class together and the class took a test to determine if you were an extrovert or introvert. Margaret was around 75, a definite extrovert. I was at dead center, 50, an ambivert as I call myself - I could take people or leave them.

First semester, before Margaret and I had started seeing each other, I had applied and been accepted for summer employment at the Estes Park YMCA Camp. This was a real dilemma for me. I really had been looking forward to mountain climbing adventure, but I abhorred the thought of leaving Margaret behind. I had signed a contract and my conscience won out - I had given my word. I enjoyed mountaineering and I wrote to Margaret 4 or 5 times a week and she always replied. At the end of the summer, I wanted to get her a special present, something she would really love. I recalled that she had said she was fond of jade. I was in luck because jade is abundant in bordering Wyoming and is very inexpensive in that general area. I invested all of my lump sum tip money, $41, in a jade ring, (she would wear it every day for the rest of her life) a pendant necklace and ear rings (the jewelry she was buried in). She loved those.

I already knew I loved her very much, but I wasn't sure about her feelings for me. Soon after my return from Colorado, we had a day off at college. We went to the Nelson Art Gallery, lingered at the Chinese prayer wall, and followed with lunch at Andre's - bratwurst, red cabbage, sliced tomatoes and the best pastries on earth. Margaret was in heaven. Andre's was her favorite restaurant for all the years she had left. After that we were inseparable. Margaret would later tell me that that was the day she fell in love with me.

At mid-term our Senior year, I had had enough of college. I had purchased my own bass and three things had become obvious to me: I would never be a lawyer, or spend my life

teaching history, and I could make a living as a musician. I discussed this with Margaret and she said I should always follow my heart, the best advice anyone ever gave me. I became a college drop-out for the first time. My heart was divided. Half of it was on the road playing bass with a folk singer and the other half was back home with Margaret. I was now 22 and I began to give some serious thought about what I wanted my life to be. I wanted to be in music. but I couldn't see my life without Margaret. We'd had serious talks. We agreed we didn't want children. I wanted to continue chasing my dream and continue on as we were then, with the understanding that at some point in the future, we'd be married. Margaret wanted us to be married after she graduated. She felt that with me on the road, if we didn't get married, we'd drift apart. That spring, while I was in Stillwater, Oklahoma, playing at a real dive, I had been really thinking

about her and decided that my dream could wait. I would ask her to marry me, return to KC and get a day job. I wrote a letter of proposal from Stillwater and, to my great good fortune, she accepted. I returned to Kansas City and got a 9 to 5 day job, the only one I would have in my entire life. I became a Case Worker II at Jackson County Welfare. The salary was a pittance, but I could augment it with weekend gigs which were popping up regularly. Margaret graduated and lined up a job at the State School for the Retarded, in North Kansas City. (We had discussed possible employment and had agreed that we should both spend a couple of years doing public service jobs before moving on to our respective fields.) We were married in September of 1964 at the Eastminster

Presbyterian Church by Rev. Crockett. We moved into a small, second floor, three room furnished apartment with a Murphy bed at 515 Maple St., not far from Prospect St. and Independence Ave. I was the happiest I had ever been. Not too long after that we got our first new car, a burgundy 1965 Mustang fast-back with a black interior, a four barrel carburetor and a four speed standard transmission. She was so excited. Her Dad was a mechanic and Margaret always loved cars, and that was the first new thing of any significance she'd had in her life. It made me ecstatic to see her so happy.

As we settled into our married life, it became obvious that while we were very compatible, we were quite different in outlook. Margaret was a planner, seeing the long term, always thinking about the future. My idea of long term was next Tuesday. Jazz is a temporal art - clutching for brilliance in the fleeting instant, and then it's over. I had been unhappy enough in my life to understand that when you find happiness, you embrace it, hold onto it with all your might and you live the moment to the hilt because things can change so suddenly. Margaret wanted to save money and I wanted to spend it on high living, travel, fast sports cars and exquisite dinners. I won out most of the time. I figured that if I spent all my money, I'd just make more. For most of my life that turned out to be true. We had a grand time. Neither of us was very domestic in nature. We both were caught up in our intellectual pursuits.

A year and a half later, Viet Nam was simmering and the draft loomed. I was disgusted with my work life being what amounted to a petty bureaucrat. I called Margaret at work one day and told her that if I left that day, I could get enrolled at UMKC. Again, she said follow your heart. She said that with what she was making plus what I was picking up playing weekends, that we'd be fine. Margaret thought I should get my degree as a back-up so I did one semester as a History and Government major. Then I decided since I was never going to work in that field, that the degree was irrelevant and I became a music major (bass viol and composition) at the UMKC Conservatory of Music. Once I fully committed myself to it, it didn't take long for my career to take off. I landed a six night a week gig at the Grecian Gardens that went on for a year as I continued study at the Conservatory. Margaret had made a change also. She was following her heart as an English teacher at Raytown South High School. Then I got the break I had been waiting for all of my life. I was asked to join the Kay Dennis Show as a bassist, arranger and back-up singer, which was big time. An album, television specials, national tours and

performances of my compositions followed as I became a college drop-out for the second time. One aspect of it was perfect. Kay liked to have a steady local gig through fall, winter, and spring, then hit the road in the summer. As a teacher, Margaret was off summers, so she joined me on the road - New York, Florida, Chicago... We loved to travel and it was now being subsidized. I was surprised at what a city girl Margaret had become, for a girl who had spent the first ten years of her life in a town between two Burma-Shave signs. She really flourished in New York, visiting all the famous art galleries, seeing famous jazz artists while I was at work, - she was downright cosmopolitan. My hours were usually 9 PM till 1 AM, so we had all day to be tourists, and we were getting paid for it, seeing the Empire State Building, Statue of Liberty and the Guggenheim Museum of Modern Art... Life had exceeded my expectations and I was spectacularly happy.

While we were in New York, Margaret began having health problems, and was losing weight. Upon return to KC that fall she had a battery of medical tests and was diagnosed with ulcerative colitis, for which she took heavy medication the rest of her life.

Like most good things, after three years, that version of The Kay Dennis Show came to its double bar. Kay was interested in furthering her career, pursuing fame and fortune in Los Angeles, which paid very little money, and the band wanted to tour western Kansas where we were big fish in a small pond and could really rake in the dough. Kay went her way, moving to Los Angeles and the trio became "Ning, Roberts & Gordon" and went on playing together for 3 more years. Wanting to augment my performance income, I began to look for business opportunities. Unlike many of my colleagues, I had neither alcohol nor drug problems and could function during the day. I opened a record store, Bananafinch, which broke even for a year and a half. I closed it. Then I went into the recording business which worked quite well. Margaret continued teaching at Raytown South and became something of a rebel. All of her life she felt that teachers were grossly underpaid. She was pro-union and tried, unsuccessfully, to recruit the numbers necessary to establish a chapter, which did not endear her to the conservative to the point of being inert administration. She also decried their racial policies - segregation to the hilt! Raytown South was famous in the mid-west for being able to win basketball championships without the benefit of any African/American players. She fought prejudice every chance she got. One day, at lunch, a group of teachers was making antisemitic remarks. Margaret told them she was Jewish and didn't want to hear any more of that crap, *forte* and *animato*! If you had ever seen her, you'd know how funny that was. Margaret was half Irish and half Swedish and no one would ever have believed she was Jewish. She was brave, had sacrosanct principles, and could never suffer fools.

Margaret had gotten her Master's degree with flying colors, going mostly to night school over several years.

We loved to travel and really logged the miles, San Fancisco, Los Angeles, New York, New Orleans, Boston, Washington D. C., Montreal, Quebec, Prince Edward Island…

My recording studio and music career were both doing well. Margaret was frequently at odds with the reactionary administration which was in a determined, entrenched, but losing battle to fight integration. But she was teaching creative writing and really enjoyed her gifted students. It was the best of times. I had begun to try my hand at writing and Margaret, who could really write, was very encouraging. She thought I had a flair for dialogue and that maybe I should try a screen play. But two careers and having fun at every opportunity didn't leave much time.

One day, while having lunch at Andre's, a Swiss restaurant and *confisserie,* owned by Andre Boulier who was the Swiss Consulate, I got the idea to go to Switzerland. Margaret thought that maybe we should wait a few more years and save some money first. I pointed out that we had a cache of cash in the Credit Union and, at the age of 34, it was high time we went to Europe. I won out and we were booked on a Boeing 707 to Zurich. Margaret, like people I knew who'd grown up poor, was always worried about finances. I told her with three incomes, hers, mine from music and the recording studio, that we were doing better than our peers and should start living like that. Margaret usually bought tasteful but inexpensive clothes at Montgomery Wards. I told her she should take a few hundred, go to Hartzfeld's, an exclusive, expensive women's clothier, and buy some snappy travel clothes. She did and she really loved them.

Off we went to Switzerland. (As Margaret read on the plane, I was amused by the surrounding people who were amazed at how quickly she turned the pages.) Initially, we were at a language loss. We thought people in Switzerland spoke French which we both could speak slightly, but it's 80 percent German and we knew absolutely none. We bought a translation book, and with Margaret's language skills, she soon figured things out. She was ecstatic, riding the street cars, seeing the art galleries and museums. Then at a restaurant in Lucerne, the Wilden Mann, which had served food for over 500 years continuously, over Chateaubriand for two, she told me that this was the high point in her life, she was the happiest she'd ever been. Like I said early on, when you are truly happy, you should immerse yourself in it because everything is indefinite. Her declaration would, in all too short a time, get me through the worst period of my life. The trip to Switzerland was a smashing success. We returned to the U.S., Margaret to Raytown South and me to my gig with Julie Weaver, an exceptionally talented and beautiful soprano and pianist.

Not too long after that, Margaret took more medical tests and received the devastating diagnosis of a liver malfunction, sclerosing cholangitis, which would be terminal. She had five years to live at a minimum and ten was the maximum. After the initial shock - she was only 35 - she took it well and was determined that it would be ten years and not five, and that she would really make them count. We took weekend trips to all the nearby places she wanted to see, saw all the new movies and ate at all her favorite restaurants, and she devoured books at an amazing rate, sometimes one a day. I suggested that she quit teaching and that we use our savings to take an extended vacation to some exotic place, any place she wanted . She quickly vetoed this suggestion. She loved teaching English and being with her students, so she continued to work. But further tests revealed that she had colon cancer and she was told that failure to get the recommended surgery immediately, an ileostomy with complete removal of the large intestine, would be tantamount to suicide. This was completely devastating. She dreaded the idea of having to wear a colostomy bag for the rest of her life. In her typical fashion (she was never one to wallow in self pity) she picked herself up and declared if that's what needed to be done, then let's get on with it. The surgery was in the spring and she she bounced back quickly. The nurses couldn't believe her resilience. Six weeks later she was close to being her old self. Before the new school term began, Maragaret said that the one place she had always wanted to see was London, so we booked a flight. It was a grand trip. We stayed in a really upscale hotel and made all the tourist stops. Her favorites were the British Museum (the Rosetta Stone was still there at that time) and Stonehenge. For an all too brief and shining moment, she was the old happy Margaret, riding the Tube, cabs and buses as she absorbed London.

After we returned, Margaret went back to teaching, but really began to weaken. More bad news became the worse possible. Tests revealed that Margaret had cancer of the liver and had maybe six months to live. This was particularly bitter in that the extensive, disfiguring surgery she had undergone was entirely unnecessary. The liver cancer would have killed her before the colon cancer. (Seven months after the surgery, she was dead.) At the beginning of this ordeal, I had suggested that we go to a facility that specialized in Margaret's condition to get a second opinion. The Raytown School District had gone over to an HMO called Prime Health. The doctor, Robert Ross, whom I am convinced believed he was infallible, looked Margaret in the eye and told her that there was nothing they could do in Houston (The H. D. Anderson hospital) that they couldn't do here (the HMO wouldn't pay for a second opinion). This was an absolute, appalling falsehood, but Margaret believed him. The Kansas University Medical Center was far superior in treating Cancer and it was in greater Kansas City. Margaret never even had an Oncologist! I am bitter to this day. Margaret's life was shortened by an over-confident, self indulgent doctor, playing God.

At one point I was having a problem with my right shoulder. This same doctor told me I had calcium deposits and, if I planned on continuing to play, I needed surgery. I ignored his advice, took a month off, resumed playing, and it was fine for 25 more years of constant bass playing!

Margaret tried to keep teaching, but about a month later, she came home crying and said she had to stop, she couldn't go on any more, it wouldn't be fair to the students. At this point we had a discussion about how matters would be handled. She said that she wanted to be in charge as long as she had the mental competence to make rational decisions, and after that I would be in charge and should decide in accordance with her wishes. (I followed her every directive). She soldiered on with all the grace and courage that had made me fall in love with her when I was about 13. As her condition progressed, she shunned the narcotic analgesics. She wanted to be cognizant of what was going on and to be able to enjoy her family in what little time she had left. The nurses were amazed. She died at home (her request), among her beloved books, the afternoon of Dec. 15, 1978, at the age of 36. A light went out of my life that didn't return for eight years.

I've tried not to dwell on the sadness of her death. She lived life on her own terms, never complaining, compromising only when that was the last reasonable option, and accepting and making the most of the hand she'd been dealt. Self pity was not in her DNA. For those of you who believe that there is a reason behind these things, then my purpose for the first half of my life, with my live for today philosophy, was to be her lifestyle coach because her days would be so few. It was my destiny.

For her funeral, I wrote a piece, "Requiem," that was performed by my Concert Ensemble with a friend filling in for me on bass. That was the only music played, and it will never be performed again. The funeral home had to open another room for the overflow. I bought 100 red roses, which she loved, to cover her casket and she was buried in her jade jewelry, with Rev. Crockett, who had baptized her and married us, performing the eulogy.

After the funeral, the Vice Principal, Clarence Cox, a man whom Margaret liked and respected, showed me her letter of resignation. I never had a copy and can't remember it in its entirety, but here are some eloquent, elegant excerpts that speak for themselves:

"At first I thought, why me? Then I thought, why not me?...

Don't be bitter. I'm not. I've had a wonderful life, and now, I've been given this rare opportunity to say goodbye."

I have been fortunate beyond words. I made a living at something I loved and it was never "work", I've traveled the world, and I had the rare opportunity to have had this

extraordinary person as my wife, for 14 glorious, action packed years.

Be in the moment, my friends, for like one of Margaret's favorite songs says, "...tomorrow may never come, for all we know."

Margaret

Margaret and Me

Acknowledgments

Thanks to:

Kathleen Ross and Judy Laughlin Sander (1944 - 2011) for editing

My nephew, Kevin Gogan for being my computer "ace" and my niece Joy Sander Gogan for being my cheerleader

Angela Elam of "New Letters On the Air" whose always great advice resulted in this book

Mike Scott, of Boston, Mass. My buddy of 52 years and fellow musician, composer and writer, who understands this process as well as anyone that I know

Terry L. Roberts, my brother, for his great memory, willingness to help and to share his colorful life

Jim Sander, my friend of 60 years and my brother-in-law for 48 years for his memory and help

My niece, Amy Sander for the cover design

My niece, Jeannine Byrd Buford for photography

Made in the USA
Lexington, KY
03 April 2014